Dedicated to my beach loving, Cornish grand-daughters, Amelia,

Abigail and Imogen, with all my love.

CHAPTER ONE

A CORNISH SPRING

The blood pounded in his ears as he ran through the cobbled streets

of Mevagissey. His breath came in ragged gasps, and he knew he

was running for his life. His very existence, and all that he held dear

depended upon how far his legs could carry him, and how fast he

could run. He stumbled through the doorway of the Fountain Inn.

The overwhelming smell of tobacco and ale engulfed him, wildly

he gesticulated to the door behind him. Wordlessly the landlord

crashed down the foaming pots of ale and pushed his way through

the drunken throng, to hold open a narrow door at the back of the

tiny room. Every man in the pub knew that the alley outside, Shilly

alley Op, led up through the line of tumbledown cottages which

clustered around the harbour. Many of the cottages had been built

with fish cellars underneath, where a man could disappear among the

tangle of seine nets and fishing gear to stay hidden until the coast

was clear.

Matthew scrambled through the back door of the pub, only to fall head first into the waiting arms of the Press Gang. His life in Cornwall, in his beloved Mevagissey had ended for ever.

Matthew Hunkin was an ancestor of mine, and his story is part of my story, even though our stories are hundreds of years apart we are bound together. Bound, not only by blood, but by a genetic inheritance which reaches out across the world, calling to those whose roots have sprung from this ancient Celtic land of sheltered coves, and towering cliffs, wild moors and hidden creeks. A land, almost surrounded by sea reaching out into the Atlantic Ocean, with its own language; a land which was known in ancient times as Kernow, Cornwall.

MY STORY

I thought of Matthew while the storm raged all night.

The same screaming howling wind would have kept him awake all those years before. He would have been huddled in the family cottage, head to toe with his older brother Sam. They would have dashed from their beds down to the quay to check on the family lugger straining at her moorings, their shouts echoing around the harbour as they struggled to secure the Mildred, the families most valued possession.

The wind raced up our farm lane tearing at the windows and screaming around the ancient cob walls of our home, Church Park. It sounded desperate to get in and whisk us away from our warm beds up towards the clay hills of St Austell. Down in Portmellon, the cove below, we could hear the relentless pounding of the waves as they roared straight in, battering the ancient row of cottages which stood valiantly facing the onslaught of the sea.

I thought of Mevagissey harbour. I knew that the fishing boats would all be tucked safely into the welcoming arms of the inner harbour, while the biting easterly wind shrieked around the narrow streets, and the owners of the cafes and pubs around the quay lay anxiously in their beds dreading what damage the morning would reveal.

The storm finally ceased in the early hours and we all dropped off to sleep. We awoke to a new world, and as so often happens in Cornwall, nature throws her wildest weather at the inhabitants then suddenly reappears wearing her most benign face with a calmer sparking sea, and a bright warming sun

After the wildness of the night, the morning which greeted us heralded the beginning of a Cornish spring.

It had been a long winter, pregnant I had grown to an impressive size easily able to balance a cup and saucer on my bump and progressing to a tea pot and plate of biscuits, (well it felt like that.)

The arrival of unexpected twins had been quite a shock not only to us, but also to Bess, our old farm dog who could not make up her mind which pram to sit under when a baby began to cry.

I seemed to be surrounded by small helpless creatures, and one day when Rob rushed in from lambing carrying a tiny shivering orphaned lamb I was not impressed.

'What am I going to do with it?' I asked.

'Just wrap him in a towel and pop him in the bottom of the Rayburn, leave the door open, he'll come around in no time.'

He produced a huge bottle of milk and rushed out of the door. I was left holding yet another baby. I followed instructions and settled my new charge in the warming oven he looked comfortable and closed his eyes. Then I heard a bark from the sitting room, it was Bess telling me that one of the twins was awake. I began to warm their bottles, oh well I thought, what's one more bottle, at least I won't be changing his nappy.

Like the twins, when he woke up, the lamb attacked his bottle with gusto. I began by feeding him on my lap, but by the second feed he was much livelier and insisted on standing while grabbing the bottle in a vice like grip. From a frozen, half dead little creature when he arrived, by the evening he was tottering around the kitchen nudging me to produce more milk.

I was amazed at his powers of survival, we went to bed that night only to be woken by the sound of three babies crying for their bottles. The problem was that Larry, as we christened him began to think that he was a dog, and was soon heading for the sitting room intent on becoming one of the family. Rob decided that it was time for him to rejoin the flock, he could see that I had formed an attachment to Larry and being a true farmer he had visions of a huge sheep jostling for position in front of the fire.

I tried to dissuade him, promising that we would keep Larry outside but we both knew that I would never have kept to it, so eventually I gave in and bid Larry a sad farewell. It did put me off lamb chops for quite a while.

The great storm had been winters final attack, spring had been waiting in the wings, and burst dramatically upon the scene. A Cornish Spring is like no other, always early, the sleeping earth finally begins to wake up. The daffodils suddenly burst out from their winters sleep, their golden trumpets waving proudly, signaling that winter has been banished, to be replaced by the magic of nature and eternal life.

The daffodils are not content to be confined to gardens, over the years they have escaped from the flower farms, and appear randomly in hedges along the winding Cornish lanes. They also produce great seas of yellow beside main roads, letting everyone know that winter is officially over.

The great gardens of Cornwall really come into their own now, the camellias and rhododendrons all begin to burst into bloom. I often think of the original plant gatherers from the great estates who made it their life's work to travel all over the world and to bring back the amazing collection of exotic plants to Cornwall's welcoming climate. I wondered if they realized as they hacked their way through jungles and climbed mountains, what a lasting legacy they were handing on for future generations to enjoy.

The balmy spring weather raised my spirits, and gave me the chance to get the twins out into the great big world. They had been born in February, not the best time to come into a cold Cornish world. Down in the cove below us, the angry sea roared up onto the road stopping drivers in their tracks as they attempted to get across to Mevagissey. The cottages behind the sea road had been rebuilt after the great storm, and now put up their shutters as soon as the waves began to pound against the sea wall.

Having been confined indoors since the twins were born, the appearance of the sun and the sound of the birds busily nesting in the trees leading up to Church Park convinced me that the time was right to introduce the twins to the big wide world and their Cornwall.

I would load them into the double pram, and head down to Hitler's Walk.

Situated above Mevagissey, this is a steep park which has the most stunning views of the harbour and coastline, stretching right up to Rame Head. Curious about the name of this idyllic park, I discovered that during the second world war the home guard had used this area to patrol, watching for enemy air craft or hostile shipping.

'You could see Plymouth burning,' one old soldier told me and his words brought a chill to my heart, having been born in Plymouth I knew the devastation which had been wrought upon the old city. It must have been terrible to have to stand and watch the red glow in the sky, and to know that lives were being lost, and that the future was looking very grave for the whole country

I discovered that the name, 'Hitler's Walk' had been based on a small bossy character who lived at the top of Polkirt hill, and who would march up and down telling everyone what to do and when to do it.

Some bright spark with the Cornish love of nick names, probably one of the home guard, christened the little park, 'Hitler's Walk' and the name stuck. With the usual knack for language, Hitler's Walk, had made a kind of mockery of the situation, and even if he had invaded I wouldn't have given much for his chances down here in Cornwall, 'Trelawney's Army', would have sorted him out.

When you produce twins, you become a walking attraction, the afternoon parade was always a very sociable event. Bess would accompany the pram keeping a watchful eye on the proceedings, sinking gracefully to the ground at each stop, while I chatted to various friends and neighbours.

I never made it down Polkirt Hill into Mevagissey itself because the hill leading down into the village was narrow and very steep. The twin pram was wide, and as the twins began to eat for England, it became heavy.

This meant that I was relegated to pushing along the top road, and then into Hitler's Walk.

I didn't mind, I loved the view down into the outer harbour, there was always something going on, a fishing boat coming into land it's catch, or a visiting yacht mooring up for an overnight stay. Having checked the outer harbour I would be able to watch the activity in the inner harbour, where the grey stones of the inner quay curled around, providing a safe sanctuary for the boats, when the waves were crashing in through the outer harbour beside the light house.

Mevagissey's inner harbour had been built by those who knew the power of the sea. The boats were safe, tucked away from the force of the gales which inevitably meant no fishing, and in my grandfather's time also meant no money coming in to feed the large families, which were commonplace, my own mother was one of eight. The fishermen would have to live on tick, or hope to get a few pence pheasant beating on Caerhays or Heligan estates for the shooting parties.

Did they get offered a pheasant I wondered, or with a starving family, would they tuck the odd pheasant under their coat, or was it back to even more fish?

When I remember the stories my mother told me of those hard times, I can understand the ingenuity of those Cornish cooks who invented the Cornish pasty, a meal in its self, and the marinated mackerel, the heavy cake, and the under roast

They had to cook with the ingredients available, and stretch them for all the mouths they had to feed. I take my hat off to them.

The constant motion of the pram would inevitably put the twins to sleep and I would thankfully sink down onto one of the many benches provided with Bess collapsing beside me with a contented sigh.

I never failed to be delighted by the cottages I was looking down on. They were all different shapes and sizes lining the quay beside the inner harbour. There is an old saying in Mevagissey, where the sun shone most of the day was called 'sunny side.' The cottages are all small, and sit tucked closely together, as though hugging each other. They all have amazing views out over the outer quay and light house, towards Chapel Point. The other side of the harbour, Polkirt side, was always called 'money side'.

Built for the fish merchants, they are entirely different, lacking the spontaneity of the cottages across on the other side, and get very little sun.

Sunny side has always been my favourite part of Mevagissey. I loved to walk out onto the quay and up the path which leads under, The Oss, an old house which projects out over the path, and was built using the timbers from a ship wrecked vessel, called, 'The Horse', but always referred to by locals as the 'Oss'.

I have heard various tales about this ancient dwelling, quite a few regarding the fact that the house is haunted. The house never seemed to be lived in as a permanent home, but is used instead as a holiday retreat, yet there hardly ever seems to be visitors in it. I was told by one local that some visitors have felt uncomfortable staying there, complaining of odd sounds and doors slamming without cause. I often wondered if the fact that the old house was constructed of timbers from a wrecked ship the, Oss, has infiltrated the spirit of the place.

Maybe the souls of drowning sailors still lurk within its old walls. Recently, the Oss has been extensively renovated, when it was being done, I held my breath, would it be ruined?

Thankfully, it has retained its original appearance. The original cladding on the front of the cottage now reveals pictures of sailing ships which visited Mevagissey centuries ago, leading to the conclusion that at some time, the Oss was the harbour office, and the drawings a primitive way of keeping records.

Fascinated by the stories of The Oss, I am always happy to get to the top of the path and to lean on the wall, as fisher folk have for generations before me, and just gaze down at the boats gently rocking in the harbour below. In the summer, the quay is packed with tourists who can sit and watch the world go by, and discover the beauty of the place, while eating a Cornish pasty.

The narrow path leads on up towards the old coast guard look out, and crammed alongside are the fishermen's cottages, all of them, a lasting tribute to the ingenuity of those first builders.

They were more than just builders, they were artists, as well as being skilled craftsmen. The cottages they built stand, shoulder to shoulder, like a contingent of brave soldiers, all facing the sea, ready to do battle with the elements, and provide a haven for the brave fishermen; who sailed in their small boats, in all winds and weathers to make a living to feed their large families.

Each cottage is slightly different. Some have steps leading to a small look out, while others are larger, and have been cleverly positioned beside a smaller one.
The windows all look out to the sea, and the entire mixture of size and design are in perfect proportion.
Over the years, they have provided inspiration for countless of artists to paint, as they try to convey the beauty of the place, built hundreds of years ago, by men who possessed an innate appreciation of architecture.

At the top of the path there are two options, if you carry on you will climb up to the cliff top. Follow the path down again towards the quay and you pass a tiny cottage built for one, possibly an old fisherman who never married, and hoarded all his money under his bed.

Beside it is another larger one, always painted pink, which boasts its front door higher up the path in the roof, once again an ingenious design

There is a back door on the path going down towards the quay, which used to lead into the old fish cellar. Access into living accommodation above was up a wooden ladder, which led straight into the kitchen. This cottage was perfect for any fisherman whose boat would be moored up in the harbour below. He would be able to take off his sea boots and oil skins, store his nets and pots in the cellar, and head up the ladder into the kitchen for his tea. Altogether an ideal situation, and suitable for a bit of smuggling, if required.

Sitting on the bench in the little park looking down on Mevagissey with the twins in their pram asleep I would often day dream about my mother's village. She would always speak of it as somewhere special, sunlit days spent wandering the quay and playing truant from school. Though I was not born in Mevagissey , many of her memories have rubbed off on me.

She would often talk about the village bake house which played a vital part in my grandmother's life. Because of the difficulties involved with the old black Cornish range it was easier to just put your Sunday roast into one tin, cover it with a tea towel and carry it to the village bake house. It is easy to imagine a Sunday morning back in the old days when the wonderful smells of all the different dinners would be wafting through the narrow cobbled streets, followed by the sound of hurrying footsteps, eager to get home and settle down to possibly the one good meal of the week

. My mother could remember being given the task of collecting the Sunday roast, only to be told when she got back home, 'That's not our dinner, take it back.'

The slight problem being that my mother had already started eating one of the crispy roast potatoes on her way home. This resulted in a quick rearrangement of the dinner before being handed back.

Because times were hard, no fishing meant no money and those early mothers were wonderfully inventive in their cooking, many of the dishes resembling rustic cookery all over the world. One particular dish was a kind of dumpling wrapped in cabbage leaves, similar to the Greek dish using vine leaves. When my mother tried it at home years later, she was disappointed to find that it did not taste as good as her mother's cabbage dumplings, obviously there had been some secret ingredient which had not been revealed. Still the idea was there and we later tried it with mince and herbs which proved very successful.

Marinated pilchards or mackerel was another cheap meal.

My grandmother would pile the cleaned fish into an earthenware pot with a tight lid, add vinegar and spices, and put it into the bottom of the old range to slowly cook. This meant all the bones became soft and the fish infused with the vinegar and spices thus resembling some continental dishes which is understandable, considering that Cornish pilchards were being exported to Spain from the eighteen hundreds in huge quantities. It was big business and recipes would have travelled back to Cornwall.

Back at Church Park I was lucky enough to have a pale blue Rayburn cooker which like the old Cornish ranges, was kept going all the time providing both a warm kitchen and a marvelous drying rail, perfect for airing the hundreds of nappies.

Because Church Park was built on top of the hill between Portmellon and Mevagissey we got the full force of the wind and this proved to be ideal for the endless lines of washing clinging to the line for dear life. No such thing as disposable nappies or tumble driers for me, so it was the dear old Rayburn, and the wild wind which kept us going.

My mother came to help in those first months, and though happy to cuddle and feed the babies, she was not too keen to go out to the washing line, where you felt that you almost needed to be roped to the ground, to prevent the wind lifting you up and away over the roof tops of Mevagissey.

The Rayburn was a gift for any yeast cookery because like the old Cornish ranges it provided constant gentle heat to rise the saffron buns and cake which always played a prominent part in Cornish cookery. I always found this surprising considering the cost of saffron, 'tis dear as saffron,' was a local saying and I wondered if it was brought back by one of the trading ships and adopted in many Cornish recipes.

The fishermen had so much to contend with.

Large families to feed, the custom men hounding them, horrendous gales which washed over the quays and prevented any boats going out, and the press gangs who roamed Mevagissey's narrow streets looking for any unsuspecting fisherman to join the King's navy. I am convinced that is what happened to my distant cousin, Matthew Hunkin.

Mevagissey is full of narrow alleys, there is one secret alley I often use opposite the newsagent and behind, The Ship Inn. It is so narrow that you have to reverse if you meet anyone coming the other way, it would have been ideal for a quick get away when being chased around the maze of winding streets.

I wondered about the smugglers or free traders as they were sometimes called, the salt tax doubled the price of salt and had a huge impact on the pilchard trade in Mevagissey. Salt was the preservative which kept the fish cured and so vital for the industry. When the new tax was introduced, the Mevagissey men invented some ingenious ways of getting around the problem. They knew they had to have salt to survive. One Mevagissey man, Joseph Elvins, stated to an enquiry 'we used to tie the salt bags round the women's legs, under their long skirts, and smuggle it in.'

Salt, became as precious as brandy and silk.

Boats sailed into remote coves to be unloaded and taken into Mevagissey to layer into the barrels of pilchards caught in the bay.

So many times over the years, the Cornish have stood against injustice, beginning with Michael Joseph An Gof of St Keverne and Thomas Flamanck of Bodmin, who in 1497, marched with their

Cornish army all the way to Blackheath, to fight against paying taxes, to supply arms for a war against Scotland. They marched and fought again in 1548, this time against the King, Edward V1, who was insisting that The English Book of Common Prayer, be introduced in Cornwall, and that the old Celtic customs be stamped out.

I loved that independence which existed then, and still does now, and is ingrained into the Cornish character, 'Trelawney's Army,' we call it, when the Cornish rise up and march.

'

Looking down on the harbour I always hoped that my family had managed a bit of smuggling, enough to keep body and soul together and to beat unfair authority which would have seen the poor beaten into the ground while the rich flourished.

When you have twins however, there really is not much time for dreaming, and after a few moments of peaceful contemplation, Bess would begin to get bored, she would begin her own dreams, but not of smugglers, but of meat and biscuits, she always knew when it was getting near her tea time.

When Bess began to move, it acted like a signal for the twins who also had built in food clocks, easily activated at any time, and so we would have to leave Hitler's Walk and make haste back to Church Park.

CHAPTER TWO

SAYING GOODBYE

'All good things come to an end,' so the saying goes, and we were leaving Church Park

Rob was leaving the farm where he had worked since he left school, hoping one day to be able to get a farm of his own, but tenancies were rare, and when offered a job with the English China Clay company, he realized that a decision had to be made.

Saying goodbye is never easy, saying goodbye to the dear old house which had been our home for six years was definitely going to be a wrench. It had been such a big part of our lives, a new beginning, a new marriage and a new home in a resurrected farm house perched on top of a hill looking out over Mevagissey Bay.

Cornish life had really started here but it had only been on loan, an idyllic period when the world was new and anything was possible, having arrived with one child we were leaving with three, all in the space of six years. They had been good years, the phrase 'never a dull moment' springs to mind. The people we had met lured up our lane by my homemade, Bed and Breakfast sign, the noisy honeymooners, the naughty husband bringing first his girlfriend, and then his wife and family, the Dutch teenager with her instant boyfriend.

We had seen it all, the rich tapestry of life wending its way up to us, on the top of the hill

Now we were leaving, I knew it was ridiculous but I felt guilty, after all Church Park was only a house and we had been privileged to live there and to have been part of the restoration of the almost derelict building. Call me romantic if you like but when we first moved in and the weeks passed, I swear I could almost hear the heart of the house beginning to beat again once more. The house had gone with the job, Rob would soon be leaving the farm and we were moving back to Gorran Haven, just over the hill.

My romantic flights of fancy never have had much respect from

Rob who is a realist. Moving day was a do it yourself affair, with all our furniture being hauled out onto Rob's brother's tractor and trailer.

The last thing Rob wanted to hear was me reminiscing about houses having hearts. Also, I had the twins to organize, and who at almost two years old were busy trying to get onto the tractor determined to ensure that all their toys would be loaded in good order and ready to play with immediately we arrived at our new home.

We were moving back to Gorran Haven, about a mile along the coast.

Gorran Haven was originally a tiny fishing village, but one which in the fifteenth century boasted a larger fishing fleet than Mevagissey. A survey of fifteen seventy showed that Porth Just, which was the original name of the village, was top of the list able to provide boats and men, in the event of a Spanish invasion.

I loved Gorran Haven, with its ancient stone quay, providing a strong arm which stretches out around the beach providing welcoming shelter from the madness of the easterly gales, which can roar in at any time summer or winter.

Mevagissey of course has it's safe inner harbour plus two arms protecting the outer harbour so the fishermen in Mevagissey are well protected. Moving back to Gorran Haven I soon realized that boating is a totally different ball game.

We have always had a small boat, primarily for getting to those secret coves and doing a bit of fishing.

'We will be fine now, we can get a mooring in the harbour,' I naively informed Rob. Previously we had to keep pulling our little boat up and down the steep slip at Portmellon. Now with the harbour I assumed it would be easy, we could just pop the boat down in the water and it would be bobbing about, just waiting for us to jump aboard. How wrong can you be? This illustrates the great gulf which exists between the city girl and the local.

'It's not that easy,' was the answer, 'We shall have to wait for a mooring to become available, I shall have to see the harbour master, and we shall have to check the boat every day.'

Busy trying to fit all our furniture plus three children into a new house I carried on thinking that he was being a bit negative and that I was sure it would all be relatively straight forward. How wrong I was, by this time we had brought a heavier boat complete with an inboard engine, she was called the Maggi and the idea was to share it with Rob's brother so that there would be loads of fish for everyone. What I had not realized was that the Maggi was a wooden boat and built like a battle ship. With our other little boat the Bimby, if the tide went out, you just heaved her down to the water, and away you went; with the Maggi, if you missed the tide that was it, no amount of heaving would move her. The good news was that she was a very stable boat, the twins took to boating like ducks to water and when they dashed from one side of the boat to the other I knew that the old boat would remain resolutely up right.

'Great boat for fishing,' was Rob's comment, and he was delighted when we managed to secure a mooring in the harbour

'I just need to check the boat,' became a familiar explanation for disappearing down the hill. I learnt over the years, that this excuse for man chat was used by all the men in the village who owned a boat, regardless of whether it was actually floating or even pulled up on the slip. They would all sit on the fisherman's bench outside the Big Cellars, and talk for ages about the fishing that day, who had caught what, but never disclosing, where.

Information about the location was always top secret, and as a family we had all been warned not to reveal where we had caught a bass or pollack

.

CHAPTER THREE

GORRAN HAVEN

Gorran Haven lives up to its name.

Once a tiny fishing village, it has become a haven for so many people who have driven down Bell hill, and followed the winding road which leads to the safe sandy beach and harbour. The locals have been invaded over the years by folk who have fallen in love with the place, and who can blame them.

The beach is a picture in the summer, and to stand on the ancient grey stones of the quay, and look back at the village, and the cottages on the, Fort is a joy

The tiny church of St Just is nestled into the side of the cliff and stands sentinel above the waves guarding the village.

When there is a service at St Just, its one bell echoes across the little harbour and beach calling the people to prayer, as it has done for centuries.

The harbour is protected by an old stone quay, this was originally a wooden one and was replaced in 1888 by the then squire of Caerhays Castle, to provide a safer anchorage for the fishermen.

The quay was built on a line of rocks, and consists of one arm reaching out around the boats.

Unfortunately the friendly arm cannot contend with the wildest gales, and the boats need to be pulled up when an easterly storm roars in.

A summer morning when the boats are gently rocking in the harbour, and the part-time fishermen are shouting greetings to each other as they get ready to pretend to be real fishermen; and lying about where they caught yesterday's bass, is what Gorran Haven is all about.

The same place when an easterly wind is hitting the harbour wall and sending waves crashing over anyone foolish enough to try and make it to the end of the quay to check their boat, presents a totally different picture.

Equally beautiful but dangerous, the power of the sea is forever awe inspiring.

The old local names still are still heard and their descendants go to Gorran school at the top of the hill. There is a distinct difference between Gorran folk who were mainly farmers, and those at the bottom of the hill, the fishermen of Gorran Haven. I was lucky, having married a farmer's son, who loved the sea and fishing and who was happy to emigrate to the cove at the bottom of the hill.

Gorran Haven is a mixture of locals born and bred, and of people who spent all their holidays in the Haven and always loved the place. Once they retired, they were able to fulfil their Cornish dream, and as one full time resident said, 'even as a child I knew that one day I would live here.'

Moving to Cornwall is a big step and for some it doesn't always live up to expectations, the beach in the summer is a totally different place to the beach in the winter, with rain lashing the sand and huge waves hammering the old quay.

Then, you suddenly get a bright blue sky, the sun lights up the land, the sea changes from a cold grey to deep blue, people immerge and greet each other, 'Isn't it lovely,' or 'aren't we lucky?' and the magic of Cornwall has got them hooked .

People really appreciate good weather in Cornwall and when the sun shines Cornwall is at her very best. The light which so many artists rave about, dances on the sea picking out the different shades of sparkling azure blue and illuminating the craggy rocks and headlands.

Bad weather, also holds a dangerous fascination. Huge waves pound the sea walls and rolls onto the beaches. Wave watching is almost a national sport, and Gorran Haven beach and quay always draws the watchers.

I have seen the waves crashing over the quay, rolling up the beach, hitting the lime kiln wall and drenching the wave watchers above, who had foolishly thought that they were standing in a safe place.

Portmellon, just two miles away, always provides a dramatic spectacle, with the waves dashing in hitting the wall and being flung high in the air right over the roofs of the cottages.

This means that the road is awash, and the access to Mevagissey closed until the tide goes out.

Living in Cornwall all the year round you soon become acquainted with the state of the tide and the seasons, and very quickly learn to appreciate the power and majesty of the storms, and the fickle moods of the sea.

Weather watching, is a vital part of owning a boat in Gorran Haven. When we moved back I had imagined our days of launching and pulling up, as we had done in Portmellon would be over. We could get a permanent mooring in the harbour and life would be simple. How wrong can you be?

The mooring we were given was close to the beach, ideal, I thought but I was to be proved wrong.

The waves came roaring in, hit the quay and then rush back again. Our boat, the Maggi got all the back wash.

I thought Rob was being too fussy when he informed me that we had to watch out for any hint of an easterly and be ready to pull up. I was to be proved wrong; boats have been swamped and sunk over the years. Now as soon as a force five to eight easterly begins to blow the boat owners all rush down to the harbour, as they have done for centuries to haul up the boats. Various visitors have refused to listen to the old locals and when they see the tractors and trailers on the beach, they wonder what all the fuss is about. The sun is shining, the sea is deep blue, why are all these mad people dashing around pulling up their little boats.

Well, they find out why the next morning when the deep blue sea has changed overnight to an angry grey and the waves are rolling in and crashing into the poorly moored speed boats as they lurch from side to side and shudder at each new impact. Lessons are learnt the hard way and experience is the master of the sea.

The twins were growing up, old enough to love the boat and happy to go on trips to look for seals, as long as we could land on either Vault or Great Perhaver beach, have a picnic or build a fire and cook sausages. We had the same old situation regarding landing at Great Perhaver with waves appearing from nowhere, soggy picnics, and wet sausages, but they never seemed to mind.

Collecting drift wood for the fire was always a task eagerly accepted followed of course by the lighting ceremony. Looking for wood big enough for a table was another occupation and if anyone could add to this by finding any old oil cans for seats it was real luxury.

Simple pleasures, how lucky we were to have the beach, even luckier to have the boat, plus a mooring. True the boat was built of clinker so extremely heavy, but as Rob said, 'solid, and safe,' and it had to be, with children hanging over the side to look down through the sparking clear water for the fish swimming between the long waving strands of sea weed, as we cruised over to our Sunday beach Vault. The sea around Vault is clear a glass and the sight of crabs crawling along the sand or a huge jelly fish being washed gently by the waves, always meant hanging onto the twins for dear life as they spotted each sea creature.

After a long day at the beach loading everyone back into the boat was always a bit tricky, due mainly to the amount of equipment we seemed to travel with. Buckets and spades which were naturally a necessity, plus bathers and towels, jumpers, picnic, cricket bat and ball, shrimp nets not forgetting the dog, and a variety of children. I always say that within minutes of hitting the beach we can create a war zone as we spread around our area.

It is all very peaceful until our captain, Rob, shouts 'time to go,' and suddenly it all becomes a military operation with everyone playing their part.

The main role for the captain is to get the boat onto the beach, while the rest of us struggle down to the water's edge loaded up with all the beach equipment plus various treasures collected during the day.

I always breathed a sigh of relief when the engine kicked in and we would chug away loaded to the gunnels and heading back towards Gorran Haven harbour. The trouble was that the inboard engine we had on the Maggi was old and temperamental, one minute you would be motoring along without a care in the world the next, there would be a rattle and a sigh, then silence, leaving us drifting and at the mercy of the sea

Rob would get out his selection of plugs and screw drivers and proceed to shift everyone out of the way while he lifted off the engine cover and proceeded to coax it into starting again. We were never allowed to accept a tow, and any offers of help were always declined with a cheery wave from our mechanic, he could fix it just give him time.

Male pride is a funny old thing. I was always ready to accept the offer of a tow, especially when the kids were getting restless and at the end of the day, it seemed to me the obvious solution, but Rob made it very clear, it was not an option.

So we would sit there, rocking gently, while I would try to salvage some odd biscuits or dog eared sandwiches left over from our picnic. When the old engine finally spluttered into life, I would heave a sigh of relief knowing that Rob's honour had been saved, and we would sleep in our own beds that night.

I gradually realized that we were not alone in having engine trouble, the fishermen's bench at the top of the beach is where you get all the boating and fishing news.

This is the long wooden bench which is situated outside the Big Cellars, and where stories of engines abound, everyone at some time has trouble with their boat engine and this made me feel a bit better. I was to learn that boating is never predictable, there is always an element of risk and the unexpected

I loved the old fishermen's bench, a great meeting place for local news as well as fishing news. Gorran Haven had previously been a vital fishing cove but the numbers of full time fishermen had depleted over the years leaving just a few still making their living from the sea. Old fishermen never retire, they just get a smaller boat, and still head out into the bay to haul a few pots or to catch a bass. This is what keeps them young, you can't have Alzheimer's disease when you are motoring towards your secret fishing mark, or checking your crab pots.

Frank Guy was one of the fishermen often sitting on the bench, always smiling with a wicked twinkle in his eye Frank had weathered life's storms with a brave heart finally spending his last years in a calm harbour. He loved a joke and he loved his tot of rum, and he had an eye for the ladies, even into his late seventies he could still charm the birds out of the trees. Rob loved Frank because Frank was good enough to tell him the secret marks where he caught the biggest Pollack. Fishing marks are top secret and always have been, generally handed down from father to son.

Frank knew that Rob was at a disadvantage being a farmer's son and he took pity on him, so one sunny morning when Rob chugged into the harbour having caught no fish, dear old Frank sat him down and proceeded to tell him the secrets of the ocean.

I am not allowed to divulge these secret fishing marks and the enormity of Franks legacy weighs heavily on Rob's shoulders. When we motor back into the harbour with a good catch aboard I know it is more than my life is worth to give even a hint of where we caught them. Suffice to say that we do not rely on modern technology, lining up with various trees and rocks is as much as I can say, but it all works, plus as far as I am concerned feminine intuition which has also worked; though it took Rob a long time to admit it.

Motoring back one morning after a disappointing fishing trip I suddenly had an idea. We had tried all the usual marks, and were going to have to come into the bench with our tails between our legs. Male pride was being threatened, and fishing pride was at risk.

'Head for the Gwineas' I shouted over the chug of the engine.

'Why?' came back the reply.

'Because I have a feeling,' I said.

'Waste of time, there aren't any fish today.'

I decided to pull rank, 'I'm a fisherman's granddaughter,' I loudly informed him, 'and I know what I'm talking about.'

I pointed, 'head for the Gwineas.'

Reluctantly he changed course, I threw my line back over and hoped for the best, not really believing that it would work, then bang the line twitched hard and I knew that I had a big fish. Rob was speechless, and so was I.

It was the best feeling in the world to be able to say, 'I told you so.'

CHAPTER FOUR

BIG CELLARS

So it was back to the harbour with fishing honour restored. Luckily there was quite a gathering on the bench in front of the Big Cellars, which meant that we did not have to slink along the harbour and up the beach empty handed. Though he would not admit it, Rob enjoys being the big hunter and gatherer, and marching up the beach casually carrying some huge fish.

It is even better when visitors stop him to ask what kind of fish they are, and he can make it sound as though he does it every day with no effort at all. If they are foolish enough to ask him where he has caught them, then of course it is a completely different matter He immediately assumes his silent Cornishman demeanour and never answers, leaving me to smile politely and explain 'sorry that is top secret information,' before hurrying after him.

Honour restored we can then sit on the bench and bask in the glory. Records prove that there has been a sea fishery in Gorran Haven since 1270, for many years the fishery in the Haven was much bigger than Mevagissey.

The Big Cellars, were put there for the benefit of the fishermen, to store their nets and fishing gear, plus a pilchard press. It is one of the only authentic fish cellars left in the county.

Pilchards were the main source of income which saved the fishing communities from poverty. The old pilchard press, in the cellars, has been renovated as a lasting tribute to those valiant men who braved all winds and weathers to feed their large families.

The great wooden doors of the cellars which have only recently been replaced, were made from wood salvaged from a Russian sailing ship The Palas, which was wrecked on the rocks off Great Perhaver, the adjoining harbour beach.

This same wood was used in the cottages in the Haven, and an old fisherman in the village was the proud possessor of a fine ship's telescope

This was no story of lights on rocks luring sailors to their death. The locals did what those who live on the coast have always done, strained every effort to save the unfortunate seamen, no one was drowned and all were cared for in the village. Times were hard and it made perfect sense to salvage what they could letting nothing of any use go to waste. This proves that recycling is nothing new, why let the sea devour good wood and allow a perfectly useable telescope to rust and be broken up on the rocks.

We had also been lucky enough to have benefited from an easterly gale out in the channel. When we first moved back to the Haven a load of fine wood planks had been washed overboard, ending up on Colona beach near Portmellon. We were having an extra bedroom built to accommodate our instant family, and the planks of wood were a gift. Money was tight, and our builder was happy to use the wood Rob had salvaged from the bounteous sea.

Big Cellars, is at the back of the beach and like the fishing marks it is top secret, jealously guarded by the still thriving, Gorran Haven Fishermen's Society, there is a strict code of membership. The great doors are locked, keys are like gold dust and very few without a key ever get to see inside.

The building has been lovingly protected over the years and is now divided into, bays, for those lucky enough to belong to the society. It is full of fishing gear and a bit like Aladdin's cave, you never know what you are going to find.

Even though Rob has a key and is member, I always feel that I am an interloper when I follow him. The floor is made up of uneven cobbles and ancient wood, there are paintings of ships done on old pieces of board, and one of a buxom mermaid, donated by one of our own local artists the late, Ernest Oliver, a much loved, past chairman of the society.

It is the smell that always gets me, a mixture of old tarred nets and the endless tons of pilchards, long since gone, but interred in the very fabric of the building . The ghosts of hard working fishermen seem to hang about the place, and I am always relieved to get back outside, into the sunshine and onto the beach.

CHAPTER FIVE

GONE FISHING

So, we were fisherman or rather fisherman and fisher woman.

I guess that fishing is in my blood, and after my initial reservations about the size of the fish and the way they were dispatched we came to an agreement which involved always putting the tiddlers back, whatever the species.

With fishing quotas and regulations now highly structured we had been making our own guide lines for years

It always seemed common sense to put the small fish back giving them time to live and grow, I must admit, some of my insistence was partly due to a reluctance to take any life before it had had a good shot at the actual process of living.

Apart from the occasional moments regarding what I would call, a baby fish, we managed to agree, most of the time, and now that the twins were at school it gave us time to head out to sea and with Franks tips, begin to catch happy well lived fish.

There is nothing quite like that feeling of heading out into the bay, especially on an early summer morning, when only the small boat people are awake and eager to start the day.

When the outboard engine springs into life the look of happiness on Rob's face says it all. We are away, the harvest of the sea is calling, and as we cruise out into the bay.

I always enjoy looking back at the village as it begins to wake up. The early morning sun beginning to light up the old cottages which are clustered around the harbour, and the tiny church of St Just, watching, as it has done for centuries, those who go down to the sea in boats. The eager dog walker throwing sticks into the sea and enjoying the luxury of an empty beach, the odd visitor who has woken early and is walking along the old quay enjoying the peaceful scene, and the child on their first holiday morning, busily digging in the sand.

The first day we went fishing after Frank's secrets of the ocean, had been revealed we were full of confidence.

'Right,' said Rob, 'we have to get lined up.'

'Lined up?' I enquired thinking that we would need special equipment for this delicate procedure.

Rob screwed up his eyes and stared back at the land. I screwed up my eyes as well and stared into the distance. I had no idea what I was supposed to be looking for.

I was perplexed, nothing looked different.

No compass had been used, there was no piece of technical equipment, just Rob gazing into the distance.

'Is that it?' I asked, 'what are you doing?'

He was very vague with the answer and it took me years to work out what exactly was going on, and to divulge the information is more that my life is worth. Suffice to say these magical fishing marks are all based on thorn trees and certain rocks plus a church spire. I never did work it out.

We did catch fish, we always use hand lines so it is a very physical operation, no nice easy rod and reel for us. This is real fishing, a line wrapped around a wooden frame with a variety of weights and when you feel a bite you pull it all in again. Then there is always the risk of the line getting tangled up in the bottom of the boat, and spending hours trying to untangle it.

Is it worth it?

Well the answer is a resounding 'yes.'

There is nothing like the taste of really fresh fish, and knowing that you have caught it yourself, adds to the sense of satisfaction. The hunter and gatherer is still dormant in our genes, just waiting to be let out.

The good news was that having gained some of dear old Frank's fishing marks, we now knew where we were going. The added bonus, as far as I was concerned, was always the chance to come face to face with some of the other inhabitants of the sea.

Dolphins of course take the starring role, and I am always envious when people arrive back in the harbour boasting that they have just seen dolphins out in the bay. We looked in vain for years with no luck but then last summer we were finally rewarded. A large pod swam past our boat heading towards Fowey and we sat mesmerized, watching their graceful bodies swimming in perfect unison as they sped past us. It was a magical moment finally we had seen them and now we could come back into the harbour proudly bearing the good news.

Seals are great characters. There is one in particular who the local fishermen christened Samson, and who is without doubt the daddy of them all.

We often see his huge head peering at us beside the rocks on the Gwineas surrounded by his harem.

He became so confident that he would cruise into Mevagissey harbour where the ladies running the fish stall would sometimes throw him any fish that was left.

When I first started going fishing I went armed with supplies, food being at the top of the list. I knew that I was in for a long haul and being out in the fresh air always made me hungry, and a good supply of coffee was a must. Long hours with nothing happening were not my cup of tea so I decided to take a book to read to pass the time. This would be after I had enjoyed the scenery on the way out to the fishing mark. We were always within sight of land, and I loved the cliffs with the gulls coming into land on their chosen spots, the parents trying to take a break, while the grey speckled babies kept up a shout for more breakfast.

Gulls mate for life and are so much a vital part of the Cornish scene I cannot imagine our cliffs without the sight of those white wings riding on the air currents or coming into land on precarious ledges. The shags and cormorants are also an act of their own, shooting out of the sea to perch on the rocks with their wings out stretched to dry, all lined up like soldiers on parade

Once out in the bay and past the cliffs, waiting for a bite can be a bit tedious, so I decided to crack the boredom problem by taking a book to read. The first time I was full of confidence. I slung out the line, got out the coffee, produced my book and relaxed, or so I thought. After a few minutes my line twitched, I could not believe it, surely I had not caught a fish so soon.

I pulled in the line, Rob fishing on the other side of the boat was just as surprised as I was.

I pulled in a good sized pollack, I must explain at this stage. I pull them in, then Rob takes over, getting them off the hook, and using a hammer to ensure a quick death. One of my conditions for going fishing.

Having completed this, and then putting the line out again I settled down to my coffee, which was cold by this time.

I had another twitch on the line.

I decided to ignore it and carried on reading, but it was no good, the line suddenly felt very heavy, more twitching with a sigh I put down the book.

'You have never got other one,' Rob said, looking amazed.

'I think so,' I muttered, as I pulled in the mile long line again, 'you had better get the landing net.'

This time the fish was a beauty, and I was impressed myself, I had never been so successful.

Rob was beginning to wonder, what was the secret of my success.

I must admit I was wondering myself.

I had one more go at reading my book but had to give it up. I just kept catching fish. Rob was pleased, but I could see from his expression that he was finding it all a bit much, especially as I did not help matters by saying, 'Not another fish, I am trying to read my book.'

I was really beginning to enjoy my experience of girl power. The more fish I was hauling in the longer Rob's face became, he was not catching at all, and the temptation to gloat was too much for me. 'I do not know what all the fuss is about,' I said.
'I guess some of us just have the knack.'

I was certainly, pushing my luck, but I couldn't resist it, eventually Rob saw the funny side, and was man enough to accept that I was a serious contender for catch of the day.

This did not always happen, but I usually managed to come back to the little harbour with a few reasonable fish, thus almost making me one of the gang, but not quite.
I was a woman after all, but at least the other fishermen acknowledged my existence, and when sitting on the fishermen's bench I was allowed to join in the endless conversations of who caught what and where.

The bench serves as a meeting point, not only for catching up on the fishing news, but also village affairs.

A walk down into the village is never complete without a quick gossip on the bench, which provides a marvellous panorama of everything happening on the beach. Because we have two village beaches, plus the harbour, there is always something to watch.

The state of the sea is one topic which never fails to be discussed, the moorings also provides great scope for detailed analysis, and the sight of visitors backing their boats down the slip, will stop everyone in their tracks, until the procedure has been successfully completed. If a visitor gets stuck then the locals will help, but not until they have gained the maximum entertainment from the spectacle. There is an undying delight in watching other boaters getting it wrong, or being beaten by the unpredictability of the sea.

Falling into the sea happens to both visitors and locals alike, and you always hope that the audience on the bench have missed the event. The truth of the matter is that you can bet your bottom dollar you will have been seen. Someone will have spotted you immerging from the water dripping wet, and the bush telegraph will swing into action. Within a few hours all the beach community will know what has happened and the jokes will come fast and furious.

Gorran Haven Fisherman's Society is a vibrant strong

organization, and at their Annual General Meeting there is always an award for the best cock up of the season. This can range from falling in, to hitting the quay while trying to moor up, or even to dropping the catch over board, the list is endless.

This accolade is not one that any of the boys want to win, but is always taken in good humour, or seems to be to save face.

They say that pride comes before a fall and I experienced this one summer evening after a successful fishing trip. Rob was mooring up the boat and I was delegated to row our new punt in onto the beach. 'It is easy to row,' Rob informed me, and we loaded the punt up with all the fishing equipment and I set off feeling very important, I was in charge. He was right, the little punt was a joy to row, nothing to it, I headed for the beach and confidently pulled in beside a family group enjoying the last rays of the sun. I shipped the oars and slung one leg out into the water

Unfortunately I was used to our other boat and I had not bargained for the lightness of the new punt. The whole thing tipped up depositing me and all the gear into the water.

Luckily it was only waist deep. I floundered about, all dignity gone, soaking wet I chucked everything back into the boat and pulled it up onto the sand'

The visitors sat open mouthed. No one said a word, I gave a nervous grin and stalked up the beach and out onto the quay where Rob was merrily mooring up the boat

He completed his task and climbed up the ladder onto the quay, 'you are quiet,' he observed as we marched along, 'no wonder' I answered, through gritted teeth, 'I have just fallen in, you did not say how easily the punt tips up.'

He stopped walking and surveyed me, 'Yes you are looking a bit wet.'

He began to laugh, but managed to contain it, 'better get home, good job its warm.'

  I knew that someone would have seen me and the jokes continued for a few weeks, every time I put on my bathers some bright spark would shout,' you don't need them, just stick to the jeans and jumper.'

This went on until someone else made a boob, and I was off the hook.

CHAPTER SIX

FISHING CHARACTERS

While Frank continued to charm the ladies, Dick Pascoe became the proud owner of the Buccaneer, and began taking out fishing trips around the bay.

Frank epitomized the small sturdy Celt.

Dick was the complete opposite. Big in every way, over six foot, he was an imposing figure striding down the beach. Originally a fisherman, he now had to charm the many visitors who flocked to catch the silver mackerel jumping in Mevagissey bay.

Blessed with a wicked sense of humour Dick would enjoy spinning the odd yarn to entertain the visitors and himself.

Chapel Point, between Gorran Haven and Mevagissey always produced questions from the trippers, 'who lived in the amazing turreted castle like buildings, perched on the private headland?'

Dick would explain about the architect who lived in a hut on the cliff while the houses were being built.

But there was more, as the boat edged in closer to the small beach the crew would be even more intrigued by the sight of large animals standing in the water.

The fields on the point belong to Bodrugan farm and on a hot summers day the cattle often make their way down the valley to the beach to indulge in a spot of paddling.

'What are they?' an American tourist asked Dick as he negotiated the Buccaneer close to the headland.

'Water buffalo,' Dick replied.

'Water buffalo,' the tourist was impressed.

'Yes, they are the last herd in England, down here in little old Cornwall.'

'Wow,' the American was hurriedly taking out his camera, 'Can we get a bit nearer?'

'No this is as close as we can get, they could stampede.'

Dick opened out the engine and the boat steamed on with everyone on board straining their eyes to see the last herd of water buffalo left in England.

Trips down the coast always included the towering highest point in Cornwall, the famous Dodman. The scene of many ship wrecks over the years the Dodman stretches out beside the golden sand of Vault beach shielding Gorran Haven from the South winds. Crowned by a huge granite cross, erected by a previous vicar of Gorran, the Dodman is a mighty sight from the sea and land.

Dick would always relate the true story of the paratroopers who practiced scaling the Dodman during the second world war. 'They could get to the top in ten minutes with all their packs on their backs,' he would inform the incredulous visitors craning their necks up the cliff to see the granite cross on the top.

Then he would enjoy embellishing the tale.

'Of course, the Cornish Pioneer Corps tried it and nearly got to the top in eight minutes.'

The crew looked suitably impressed, 'What happened?' would always be asked.

'Well the problem was, they ran out of scaffolding,' Dick would answer keeping a straight face.

Dick later became the harbour master, a role which required interaction with both the full-time fishermen and the increasing number of part timers, plus the visitors who drive down to Cornwall pulling a variety of small boats behind them. The part time fishermen always feel superior to the visiting boaters, simply because the locals know the problems that the sea can throw up. Weather watching is an art in Gorran Haven, listening to the forecast, and then adding your own interpretation is an important pass time

The old bench outside Big Cellars is always the focus of weather news, and the inevitable decisions 'shall we pull up or leave her down.'

I have always been an advocator of leaving her down.

That is until an easterly suddenly blew up becoming stronger than I had bargained for. We lay in bed listening to the increasing howls of the wind, and I knew that I had got it wrong.

Rob, who always errs on the safe side and who loves his boat more than wife or kids, finally jumped out of bed in a complete panic. We can see the Gwineas from our house, a group of rocks which can be used to judge the state of the sea.

'It's coming over the Gwineas,' he yelled, pulling on his jeans,'I told you we should have pulled up.'

There was no answer, I jumped out after him and began to wake up Michael and Vicky, still half asleep we rushed down to the beach. My heart dropped as I saw the huge mountainous waves washing over the quay. Our boat, the Maggi, was wallowing in the waves. The mooring we had then was close to the beach, but it suffered from the back wash as the waves hit the beach, the boat was full of water.

Rob dashed into the sea and began bailing her out, Michael waded out to help him and Vicky and I watched from the beach.

A visitor's boat, moored out further than ours had gone down and the whole scene was one of chaos.

The Maggi survived on that occasion, and lived to fish another day, but she was an old wooden boat, pulling her up required a winch and eventually we got rid of her and acquired a lighter fibre glass boat which was called appropriately, 'Trouble Maker.'

We also finally got a better mooring, tucked inside the corner of the quay.

This mooring is safe through most gales, that is, until the waves wash right over the top of the quay, and then you know it is time to get out.

We kept the name of the new boat, because it is bad luck to change a boats name and we still have it.

Rob and Trouble Maker seem to go very well together.

CHAPTER SEVEN

CORNISH   CULTURE

Many people who come to Cornwall are fooled by the sheer distance from London and the rest of the world. They imagine that culture remains the prerogative of London and the big cities, but once down here, they realize how wrong they are. Cornish culture is alive and thriving, music is a vital part, our choirs and brass bands are an integral part of Cornish life.

The Tate at St Ives has shone the spot light on Cornish art, but long before the establishment acknowledged the value of Cornish artists, the Newlyn school was thriving with artists from all over the world descending onto the little fishing village of Newlyn anxious to record the fascinating lives of the fishing communities.

Here in Gorran Haven we suddenly got more than our share of culture, when a slim, motor bike riding teacher, arrived up at Gorran Primary school. Because the school was the focus of the community, his arrival became the subject of much interest. Just qualified, and full of enthusiasm, possessing an innate connection with the children, Mike Shepherd was an instant hit. The kids loved him for his great sense of fun and the mums just loved him.

Mike's parents had moved to Cornwall from London, in the days when the journey took long hours and Cornwall seemed to be at the end of the world. Mike had enjoyed his Cornish childhood, spent making camps and climbing trees, and eventually followed his father into the teaching profession. The problem was that his heart was not really in it. He had a dream, and after a while we heard that he had given in his notice at the school to follow that dream and to bring theatre to Cornwall

The locals heard this news with a certain amount of scepticism. This was Gorran Haven, theatre did not really exist down here, we got the school Christmas play and pantomimes in St Austell but we were just a little village on the coast.

The whole idea seemed pie in the sky, 'he's got a good job up school what is he doing this for?' was the general consensus of opinion. Mike carried on regardless, managing to rent a barn up on the hill and collect together an assortment of like minded individuals, 'all a bit way out if you ask me,' one local observed, 'what are em like for goodness sake?'

Then a notice went up at the school, 'Kneehigh' were going to perform a play for both parents and children. The kids were delighted, they knew their ex teacher, it was bound to be good. The parents were less enthusiast, they had no idea what to expect and what kind of name was 'Kneehigh?

We all gathered at the allotted time in the school hall.

Suddenly there was a bang and a crash, everything was happening, it was the kind of theatre which interacted with the audience

There was fake smoke filling the room, the odd monster, excitement building to an amazing finale. The energy was palpable you could not help but be washed along on a wave of delight.

Kneehigh had arrived in our midst and continues to this day, the barn has expanded, the company is now performing all over the world, enjoying hits on Broadway and the London stage.

Mike Shepherd is still at the center of the company, still performing and passionate in his love of Cornwall and local theatre. What an achievement for a local boy who had a dream and has altered the face of live theatre in the county for ever.

Whenever the company comes home with a production, they are guaranteed full houses, their reputation ensuring an enthusiastic welcome from both visitors and locals alike, who regard Kneehigh as their own.

Their return to Cornwall is always eagerly awaited.

There are no windy cliff tops or castle productions now, the company owns, The Asylum, an amazing huge dome shaped marquee, which is the height of luxury and is always packed to capacity. I can't help thinking that we were privileged to have been there, right from the very beginning.

Those early days were a jump into the unknown, based on a passionate belief that art is for everyone, not just for the chosen few. There were stories often with a political message, but done in such a creative and fun way that they appealed to one and all, much like the Cornish motto.

The company still rehearses up at the barn, and it must be a revelation for all new cast members to find themselves perched high on a Cornish hill top, with the sea and the great stretch of Vault beach below them.

Theatre was not on Rob's list of things to do, and my visits had been confined to trips to the pantomime in Plymouth and the odd trip to the ballet with my god mother. I wondered how I was going to get Rob to join us when Knee High was performing, I felt sure that he would enjoy it if only we could get him there.

Then I realized that I had one great advantage, Mike Shepherd was a cricketer this immediately transformed him from an arty farty actor into a real man, or so Rob thought. The fact that Rob was now the captain of the cricket team, and Mike was always ready to turn out if he was home, and just as passionate about cricket as Rob meant that the two bonded

This meant that we could haul Rob to performances which in the early days were on cliff tops, in castles, in some of our great gardens, and village halls.

He found to his surprise he really enjoyed these startling performances, theatre had truly arrived.

The interesting thing was that cricket still took top billing, when Mike arrived home from on tour all he wanted to hear about was how Gorran Cricket team was getting on, 'You have to get your priorities right,' I was informed.

CHAPTER EIGHT

THE CRICKET DINNER

Before I arrived in Cornwall Annual General meetings were not part of my life, staff meetings yes, but A.G.M.s as they were called meant nothing to me. Having been voted onto the tea committee at the cricket club I felt privileged when Rob suggested that I attend the A.G.M. with him

I arrived back home in a state of shock, somehow I had been voted in as the secretary of Gorran Cricket Club. I was still not sure exactly how this had happened. Number one, the secretary had always been a man, and number two, I was just at the stage of understanding cricket, plus Gorran was an important club in the league, how would a mere woman fulfil this hallowed position

   I later found out that the reason I had been handed the mantle was because that particular year the committee had been desperately searching for someone to take on the role. Not expecting to be taken seriously, I had said innocently, 'I will do it for a year, if no one else will.'

Big mistake, I ended up doing it for twelve years and it finally dawned on me exactly what A.G.M.'s were about, to get you aboard, my advice 'don't go.'

So I became honorary secretary of the cricket club, and luckily I had Rob at my side to keep me on the straight and narrow. Cricket is Rob's main reason for being alive in the summer and I was working on the theory of 'if you can't beat them, join them.'

This resulted in many hours spent watching cricket and of course, as any cricketer's wife or partner will tell you, doing the teas.

   After doing the job for five years I felt that I had got the hang of it, but there had been a few near misses along the way like my first cricket dinner, when I reckoned I was well organized

All the cups had been engraved, the venue booked, and everyone managed to be at their appointed places along the route. We were off into the big lights of St Austell and I was on a roll, or so I thought.

Once we got to the top table I was seated beside the president of the club, Mr Julian Williams of Caerhays castle with the vice chairman of the club on my other side. I was not in the habit of making polite conversation with owners of castles and the vice chairman, my friend John Vercoe, proceeded to oil the waters, so to speak by liberally refilling my wine glass throughout the meal.

As the dinner progressed I was mentally patting myself on the back, nothing to it I thought as I surveyed the diners through a rosy glow of satisfaction. The dinner was over, coffee was being served, I began to relax. The president had confided to me that he never really enjoyed his dinner at these functions because of the thought of making a speech at the end. Poor guy I thought, completely forgetting that my role in the proceedings was not yet complete.

The speeches all ended and I could see Rob's face peering at me from further up the table, 'and now we shall present the cups' said the chairman, turning to me.

I had organized a trophy table and put the cups on it thinking that was it, but no, I was expected to go up with the president and chairman, and hand the cups to the president, who would then present them to the to the appropriate players.

Simple, I sailed up to the table full of confidence, as each name was read out I picked up the nearest cup and handed to the president with a flourish. I was on a roll, and full of good will towards the world. Rob's face was a picture, he could see that I was grabbing cups with gay abandon.

The most improved young player got the first team batting cup, the second team's bowling cup went to the best fielder and so on. I was totally oblivious to it all handing out cups left, right and center, I was having the best time. The players were understanding, I think that they were aware that their secretary had partaken of too much wine, and so they quietly sorted it out later. The evening continued to flow, and a good time was had by one and all. The coach turned up at mid night and Rob herded everyone into the bus and we set off back to Gorran Haven.

Getting every one, into the coach for the homeward journey always proved tricky.

Some seemed bent on extending their stay until the early hours, while for the rest of us, like Cinderella when the clock struck midnight, it was time to go.

The coach rumbled on and I settled down in my seat planning a snooze on the way home, then there was a shout from the back of the bus, some of the ladies desperately required the loo. The driver always willing to oblige a lady thoughtfully, pulled in on the corner close to the entrance of Heligan Gardens, where there is a small triangle of grass and trees affording a certain amount of privacy. The ladies, all still in high spirits trooped off the bus in their long ball gowns and vanished among the trees. Looking out of the window I could see that privacy was not high on their list of priorities, there were shrieks of laughter and one got stuck in a bramble and had to be rescued by a gallant cricketer. The rest eventually managed to stagger back onto the coach, we all heaved a sigh of relief and rumbled on. By this time we were close to Gorran Highlanes, not far to go.

Then another shout, this time from one of the younger cricketers, Rob's nephew, was standing in the isle looking very green. 'I feel sick,' he mumbled, 'need to get out.' The coach came to a screeching halt and the lad vanished into the darkness. We waited, no sign of him, 'I better go and find him,' said Rob and he too vanished out of sight.

Once out in the darkness he was surprised to hear Phil's voice calling, but there was no sign of him.

'Where are you?' Rob yelled.

'Here,' came the reply.

The sound was coming from the field below, there is a high stone wall which runs along the road leading into Gorran.

'What are you doing down there?'

There was silence then, 'I lost my teeth, so I had to jump down to get them, now I can't get up.'

Rob leant over the wall and hauled him up.

'What took so long?' I enquired when they both returned to the coach.

'He lost his teeth.'

'What, how did he do that?'

'Well, he leant over the wall to be sick, and bang his front teeth flew out and dropped down into the field below, but once he got down there he could not get up.'

'I didn't know that he had false teeth,' I said, by now wide awake.

'They were knocked out in that cricket match,' Rob airily informed me 'still he's got them back now, no harm done.'

'Well I think losing your front teeth is quite a bit of harm,' I commented.

Cricket can be a dangerous game I thought as we were pulling into Gorran to let some revellers get off, and even the annual cricket dinner should have carried a health warning it had certainly been an eventful trip, but at least everyone was home in reasonable condition, teeth and all. I heaved a sigh of relief.

CHAPTER NINE

FAME AT LAST

One sunny morning I August I answered the telephone to and received an amazing request.

'This is Country File calling, we have heard that Gorran is in the final match of the 'Village Cup Competition,' and we are planning a programme on the event could we get together and discuss this?' Now, having various friends whose sense of humour would quite easily lead them to trying something like this I immediately began to laugh.

'Yes, what a great idea, I really fancy myself on the television.'

There was a brief silence at the other end of the phone.

'Great, when can we meet with you?'

'Oh I don't know, maybe next week,' I answered, playing along.

'Fine, we shall need to meet the captain and possibly some of the players, can we fix a time and date, and Rupert Segar will be the presenter'.

Realization began to dawn, this was not a joke this was for real. We arranged a date and the more we talked the more excited I became.

We were going to be on Country File and if we won the final, then we would be going to play at Lords, the hallowed ground of cricket, in addition, Country File, wanted to film us. It did not get much better than this.

I began ringing around, the cricketers were very laid back, the match would be the important thing, being on T.V. was not top of their priorities. However, they were good natured about the whole filming process.

The producer was a woman, and she soon had them eating out of her hand, even to the extent of being filmed running along the beach a bit like the film, Chariots of Fire.

We could hardly believe our eyes, it was a sight to behold, the only difference being that the runners in the film were top athletes, and some of our boys had definitely had too many Cornish pasties. Still the effect was there, and as the great day got nearer the excitement reached fever pitch.

The ladies also had their part to play, I had been assigned the job of organizing the tea list, and we had been filmed preparing the teas from every angle. Various people had done interviews and we were all becoming old hands at this T.V. thing.

The day finally arrived, the sun shone, the cameras began to roll. The arrangement was that the tea ladies would be filmed preparing the teas, and then each one would be asked to make a small comment about the effect cricket had on their lives. I waited while my friends all dutifully gave their answers.

'You can't go on holiday in the cricket season.'

'You can't get married in the cricket season.'

'You can't give birth in the cricket season.'

I listened to all this with growing alarm, they had said it all, what was there left for me to say.

I could see my moment of fame vanishing out of the window, I had to come up with something really different. My mind was in a whirl, then I had it.

'Now Sue, what does cricket mean to you?'

'Well, it means that you can't have sex before a match, and you certainly can't have it after.' I said laughing, thinking, no way would that comment go on a Sunday show.

The silence was deafening, I could see my friends amazed expressions, did she really say that, on Country File, it was the one programme on which the S.. word had never been heard.

The director also looked slightly stunned, but carried on sweeping the camera to the impressive array of sandwiches and cakes laid out before her.

I began to feel that my sense of fun had overstepped the mark. then the excitement of the match outside took over, we were winning.

Werrington had batted first and, had only made 154, we were definitely in with a chance. I was sure that they wouldn't use my jokey, comment, it said purely in fun, and in the heat of the moment.

So I forgot about it; outside the match was coming to an exciting final, it was a very close thing, the last ball was bowled and we won on the final two runs.

We all cheered with delight, the team we had been playing were a much bigger side in Division One, with a pavilion which had cost fifty thousand pounds. They were not like us a small village side, but trawled a large area for players, and when interviewed on television they had given the impression of quiet confidence. The presenter had described the match as David and Goliath and now David had won. Already we were planning our trip to the hallowed cricket ground at Lords we were on a roll.

Then the captain of the other side began a deep discussion with our jubilant captain, Robert Daniel, what on earth was going on? Robert was looking very serious, the rest of the players paced the ground, then finally we got the news, Werrington had looked through the small print and made a formal complaint against our selection.

One of our players had not played in eight matches in the preceding two seasons, he was a local lad and only made seven runs, but this meant that on a technicality Werrington were pronounced the winners.

So that was that, our excitement quickly turned to dismay it had been a genuine mistake, we would not be going to Lords after all. The presenter Rupert Segar had to quickly change his final summing up and his words left no doubt as to his opinion of the result.

Gorran still celebrated, a win is a win, and we thought our boys had given their all and done us proud. The weeks went by, there were other cricket matches to win and then one Sunday in the autumn we all sat down to watch Countryfile. The cricket field looked beautiful, the boys all played their hearts out and the shots of running on the beach were impressive, *more importantly,* we knew that we had really won.

Then we got to the interview with the tea ladies, I held my breath. Then there I was, large as life, a big grin on my face, saying those very unladylike words, for all the viewing public to hear.

I was mortified, what on earth had possessed me, why did I do it? Rob was struck silent for a minute, we looked at each other and began to laugh.

'That is probably the first time they have had a sex fiend on Country File,' he said.

I could not believe it, there it was for all the world to see, over the next few weeks other secretaries of many different clubs would ring me up, and their first words were always about that interview, I knew that I would never live it down.

It did do one good thing however, it made me understand the emotions behind the quest for fame, I can see now why people do it. It also taught me something else, to be sure to keep a grip on my sense of humour, it can get me into a lot of trouble.

CHAPTER TEN

A CAT CALLED THOMAS

When we moved from Church Park not only did we have to organize all the toys and furniture we also had to deal with Bess, the old farm dog who had been born out on the cliffs in a badger's den. Because she had adopted us and was now retired, and an important part of the family, when we moved to Gorran Haven, naturally Bess had to come too.

I was a bit apprehensive about moving her from the farm at Church Park where she had her own grounds to run in. Though the years spent chasing sheep and bullocks meant that her running days were over, she still did a great job, keeping the twins and I company on our afternoon excursions.

We were moving to a modern house on an estate, how would we all adapt? The house had superb sea views and once I had sold my old farm house furniture we all settled in pretty well. Bess almost immediately wandered out onto the front steps flopped down in the sun and took up residence.

The twins were walking now and the days of accompanying the big pram were over. I think she felt that she had completed the hard bit, now she could relax and spend sunny days out on the top steps snoozing in the sun.

She was becoming very deaf and when it was time for her tea, I would have to go to her and touch her on her shoulder to get her to come in.

Its amazing how those years between babyhood and big school seem to fly by.

When the twins were babies and I was immersed in the round of nappies and feeding plus the broken nights, I never imagined how quickly life would turn the pages and suddenly they were off to big school, at the top of the hill, while Christopher was off to the Roseland School, at Tregony.

Getting ready for school was always a challenge as any parent will know, children will inevitably find something vital that they need to do before being bundled into the car

I have a friend who running late, dashed out to the car, drove up to the school, turned to tell the boys to get out of the car, only to find that the car was empty, the boys were still at home.

One bright sunny morning we were all dashing around getting ready for school, 'you get in the car, I'm on my way' I shouted.

'Mum hurry up,' it was Michael's voice calling.

I rushed out of the door to be confronted by two very excited faces.

'What's all the fuss about?' I asked.

'Look,' this time it was Vicky, 'look there is a cat in the car.'

'There can't be,' I replied, 'the cats in the sitting room asleep.'

Then as I unlocked the car door I was amazed to see a tiny black face peering back at me from the front seat.

I was nonplussed for a moment, how on earth could a cat get into a locked car on our drive, all the windows were closed, it did not make any kind of sense.

'Just get in,' I said, 'we are running late.'

To my surprise the little cat did not move, just sat there while the twins climbed into the back seat and proceeded to hang over patting it.

'Sit down,' I instructed them and put the car in gear, expecting the cat to freak out at the sound of the engine. 'Can we keep it?' Vicky asked as we rattled along up to Gorran school.

'I don't know, we will have to see,' I replied, the usual answer that all parents use when really they mean 'no'.

Getting the children out of the car was not easy, they clung to it like limpets to a rock, and I had to promise that the little cat would be home at our house when they came back after school.

When Rob came home from work, I relayed the story of the cat, who by now had been given a plate of meat and was curled up beside our other cat on the settee.

We worked out what had happened.

Rob had been up to visit his parents at the farm the evening before, and it had been raining very hard and it was dark. He rang his brother to ask if they had lost a black cat.

There were always cats and kittens on the farm and Ronald was not sure but thought that it was probably one of theirs.

We concluded that when Rob had jumped out of the car, in that split second the tiny cat had jumped into a nice dry and warm environment, planning an escape from the hard toil of being just a farm cat.

Michael and Vicky were thrilled with him, our own cat was always a bit stand offish, only accepting the hugs and cuddles from the children when she felt like it, which was not that often. 'Can we keep him, please, please can we keep him?'

I looked at the tiny scrap of black fur cuddled in on Vicky's lap and realized that there was only one answer, he was going to stay

We called him Thomas, and he settled into his new home very quickly always eager to please, he endeared himself to us all even our own haughty cat Kitty Kee accepted him with resignation.

I think she was relieved to have someone who would take the cuddle pressure off her furry shoulders.

Thomas was always up for a cuddle, putting up with being lifted from a deep sleep, only to reward his small owners with his throaty purr of pleasure at seeing them.

He grew in stature, delighted to find that at this new home he did not have to catch his food, it always appeared at regular intervals, he had it made. Sometimes I thought he was suffering from an identity crisis because he loved going for walks. When we set off to take a walk along the estate and up onto the cliff path, Thomas would suddenly appear from nowhere and run along beside us. When he first started doing this we were all concerned about what would happen when we met a dog.

We need not have worried, far from running when a dog appeared, Thomas would stand his ground. Facing his adversary he would fluff up his black shiny coat, and challenge any dog to mess with him. The dogs got the message, some going out of their way to avoid him, others happy to greet him with a friendly sniff. He extended his walks as he got older, once even following Christopher when he went down onto the quay and waiting while he tried to catch a fish.

One evening when we were having a beach barbecue on Little Perhaver, Thomas strolled down Church street after me, following along the narrow cliff path and then even hopping down the steep steps to the beach behind me. The sand did not seem to bother him, he sat as close to the barbecue as possible, and demolished a couple of burgers, before curling up on one of the beach towels for a nap, and ended up being carried home due to too much food and sun.

I think he had heard that there was going to be a party, and he always loved parties regardless of the small matter of an invitation, if any of our neighbours were having a party in their garden, Thomas always put in an appearance, ready to help with any left over food which might come his way, and happy to sit on any lap available.

He always knew which day the fish van was coming and could be relied upon to accompany the van to every stop along the way, but his best adventure happened one boxing day when he arrived home with a note pinned to his collar.

'Your cat has pinched part of our cold turkey, he won't need feeding tonight.'

I looked at Thomas, fast asleep on the settee, no wonder he hadn't been shouting for his supper, I never did find out who missed out on their cold turkey sandwiches and decided that it was best to draw a veil over his latest escapade.

CHAPTER ELEVEN

A GULL CALLED SQUIRT

Living in the country you cannot help but be aware of nature which is all around you. Dogs and cats are natural pets and watching all the dogs running on the beach and enjoying swimming in the waves is a joy both to the owners and the dogs themselves. Dog walking is a wonderful way to socialize, especially in a village. We always know new people by the sight of a strange dog on the beach. Cats of course, are independent and wander around the village streets with a lordly air.

  Sea gulls, however get a bad press. The media will regularly produce wicked sea gull stories of pasties snatched from old ladies and ice creams whipped from tiny children.

I always defend them, they were here long before us, I love the gulls, their shrill sound always thrilled me when we came down to visit the family in Mevagissey, for me it was the sound of home. Buried deeply in my sub conscious was the comforting call of the gulls.

I was to discover that I was not alone in this affection because a friend's daughter who worked in Mevagissey found a baby gull which had fallen out of it's high, roof top nest.

Wendy loved all living creatures and the baby gull, a tiny ball of grey fluff was gently picked up and taken home. Luckily her parents immediately rallied around producing a cardboard box and settling the tiny bird into his new home in their kitchen.

'He has to have a name,' said Wendy's Dad, Alan, 'let's call him Squirt ' so Squirt he became, and to their amazement he flourished. Alan was one of the part time fishermen, and he began catching sand eels to feed the ever growing gull, who soon began shedding his fluffy grey baby feathers, to become a speckled grey teenage gull.

Wendy would take him for walks around the garden and he would follow her like a dog. It was agreed that because of his increasing size and sound (he would set up a shrill shout for his breakfast) he would be bedded down in the garden shed with his kitchen visits limited to the day time.

Returning him to the wild was the eventual plan and it became obvious that when he had grown and increased his speed to a run after Wendy, he would have to be encouraged to learn to fly. Wendy dedicated herself to this mission and the garden path was deemed to be ideal for the runway, hence she would dash down the path holding a mackerel behind her to encourage Squirt to finally become air borne.

Squirt however, was only interested in the food Wendy was carrying and though his feet would shoot along there was no sign of taking to the skies. Luckily Wendy did not give up, and as his wings began to expand she noticed that he would begin flapping as he chased her down the path.

Then one sunny morning when Wendy stopped running she was amazed to see that Squirt had finally made it, he was air borne, flapping wildly he soared up just missing the apple tree and landing in a heap on top of the garden shed.

The entire family were overjoyed they had done it.

Finally, Squirt would be able to fly down to the beach, and out along the harbour with all the other gulls, it was a magical moment.

Freedom beckoned and Squirt did not look back; after that first initial crash-landing he quickly worked on his flying skills until he had perfected both his take off and more importantly getting back down again. Soon he was soaring off down to the sea to mingle with the other gulls digging in the sand or just bobbing around in the harbour taking in the scenery.

By the time of the summer holidays Squirt had become a fixture on the harbour scene, when Wendy arrived down on the beach to swim, she was always accompanied by her feathered friend. Almost fully grown he would suddenly appear swooping down from his favourite perch on the harbour wall and skimming down beside her as she swam around. Visitors would be amazed to see Wendy climbing up the harbour steps after her swim, followed by a speckled grey gull who would then proceed to share her sandwiches, squawking when he felt that she was not being generous enough with his share.

Squirt grew in confidence that summer, and when Wendy's brother Ken went out fishing in the bay, Squirt would suddenly appear, swooping down to perch on the side of the boat watching the fishing with great interest. His yellow beady eyes taking it all in he would often jump onto one of the seats when Ken was baiting the line, trying to snatch a piece of tasty sand eel. Christopher used to go fishing with Ken and said that they would try to sneak out from the harbour without Squirt knowing that they had gone. Somehow this rarely worked, and when they motored out into the bay and began fishing, there would be a whirr of wings and Squirt would join them shouting loudly to announce his presence.

'He doesn't need our bait,' the boys would complain, 'he's still coming home to be fed why can't he be content with that.'
Squirt was definitely a spoilt gull.

Because he had become such a character everyone wanted to be his friend. One afternoon we motored over to Great Perhaver beach and were surprised to see Squirt winging his way towards us, he had obviously extended his perimeters and was about to join us. Unfortunately, he misjudged his landing and ended up in a heap on the wet sand, his dignity ruffled as well as his feathers.

We could not help laughing, but he quickly gathered himself together and hurried up to us afraid that he had missed the picnic, needless to say, he ended up getting nearly all my pasty.

That summer actually lived up to its name, long sunlit days and the living was easy. The beach became the focal point of our lives, the sea warmed up and stayed warm, wet suits were packed away and barbecues came into their own. Evenings after work were spent on Gorran Haven quay where luckily the sun stayed beating down on the worn granite stones.

It provided an ideal meeting place to catch up on any local news, have a swim off the steps, eat fish and chips, and drink a glass of wine in the final rays of the setting sun. Simple pleasures, but often the best, a chance to chat with friends and enjoy the beauty of Cornwall.

Squirt of course was delighted by this life style and he was keen to participate when ever he could, joining us all for a swim and happy to share our chips. All good things come to an end and after a long hot summer the chill winds of autumn are always a bit of a shock. We were reluctant to give up our evenings on the quay but finally we had to accept that our beach evenings were coming to an end, the leaves were beginning to turn brown and swimming across the harbour became more of an endurance test, winter was officially on it's way.

Squirt could not understand where everyone had gone. I would meet him sitting forlornly on the harbour wall when I took our dog Toby for a walk, and he would jump up and down wondering why there were no fish and chips or ice cream to enjoy. He was still going back to Wendy's house and being fed, but I could see that he was missing all his friends from the beach and quay, he had never seemed to bond with the other gulls, much preferring the company of humans. I often wondered if he thought he was a human because he seemed to regard the other gulls as a bit of a nuisance.

The end of this story should be that Squirt continued to grow and raise a family but unfortunately, he became rather careless. When coming into land at Wendy's house he began using the main road as a landing patch. His luck finally ran out when a car came zooming down Bell hill and ran poor Squirt over. It was a sad ending, but we consoled ourselves with the knowledge that if Wendy had not picked him up that day in Mevagissey when he fell out of his nest, he would not have had that marvellous summer we had all been lucky enough to share with him.

CHAPTER TWELVE

LOVING WHERE WE LIVE

When I first moved down to Cornwall, having been brought up in Plymouth I was not aware of the tremendous pride of place which existed in Cornwall. I was to find out that the county seems to nurture a strong deep seated sense of pride in it's inhabitants, regardless of whether they have actually been born in the place or not, it seems that the spirit of Cornwall wraps itself around the heart creating a strong desire to protect the landscape and way of life.

When the English China Clay company suddenly decided that they wanted to pipe the effluent from the clay industry into the sea off Vault beach the villagers of Gorran Haven were up in arms.
The clay industry has provided St Austell and the surrounding area with employment for generations , called White Gold, the industry boomed in the fifties and sixties and Rob later became an employee

when he left the farm. We did not know that at the time, and when I heard that there was to be a campaign to fight against the proposal, I have to admit that I was sceptical. How could a few well-intentioned villagers hope to beat such a huge industry.

Placards went up all over the village, there were petitions, jumble sales, meetings to rally everyone.

Archie Smith, born in Gorran Haven and a headmaster in St Austell, put his heart and soul into the campaign. Sir Hugh Parks, a high court judge, who loved Gorran Haven, and had a holiday cottage in the street, joined in with the locals to take on the giant clay industry. Vault beach and the Dodman Point had to be saved, the white river already flowed down the valley into the bay at Pentewan creating a wide milky blot on the sea, and the beach was more china clay residue than sand, the situation at Pentewan was bad enough now our bay was under threat.

A sponsored walk was planned and having no idea what it actually entailed I agreed to take part with my friend, Pat and her two children Ken and Wendy. Christopher was great friends with her youngest Ken and because both boys were only four years old. I had imagined that we would go so far and then drop out. The walk was to start from the car park, in Gorran Haven and then wind its way up the hill to Gorran , past the school and onto Caerhays and Trevarrick, ending up back in Gorran Haven.

We all set out at a cracking pace and it dawned on me that this was serious stuff, the march up Bell hill almost became a race and I heaved a sigh of relief when we got to the top, the children were going well and the drop down into Caerhays with the sight of the old castle and the camellias just beginning to burst into bloom was inspiring.   The tide was out and the inviting golden sand stretched away in front of us .

'Shall we stop here,' I asked Pat, 'the kids have done really well'. She looked at me as though I was mad, 'they are fine', she said and vanished up the hill in front of me.

I bent down to Christopher who was marching along beside me, 'shall we stop now,' I asked hopefully, but his little feet were already hurrying to keep up with his best friend, Ken

I realized that I had been out voted, and wearily plodded on behind them up the steep hill and on towards the little village of Caerhays. Rob had come to meet us and I gratefully accepted a lift back to Gorran Haven. Pat and the children carried on walking, determination written all over their faces arriving back in Gorran Haven to cheers from the many onlookers.

The great thing is that the campaign was a success, the proposed scheme was dropped and the sparkling blue waters of the bay remained untouched. A victory for the little man. I was to discover years later the power of the people must never be underestimated, pride of place is an awesome emotion and one which is felt with a strong passion among those who live and love Cornwall.

CHAPTER THIRTEEN

THE DODMAN

We often walked to the Dodman Point, the highest headland in Cornwall, splashing along the muddy lanes leading to the cliff path and always stopping at the old look out hut along the way. Built of stone and encased in its own garden with an old metal gate, the lookout was more of a little house than a hut, plus it had its own fire place and a window with a view of the garden. There was also an iron ring in the wall to tie up your horse, and a slate roof, so it was completely weatherproof. The children loved, the little house and we were never allowed to walk past it without paying a visit.

The questions would flow, and as the twins got older the questions became more probing,

'Why is it a look out, you can't see the sea?'

'What were they looking for?'

'Can we light a fire in the fire place?'

'Can we sleep here one night?'

Rob would generally take over the answers explaining that the men manning the little house had been watching for the free traders sailing quietly along the coast hoping to land their illegal cargoes of silk and brandy without being caught. Later the watchers would have been scanning the sea for the shoals of pilchards coming into the bay. Because it was so close to the cliff they only had to walk a few steps to check the sea, also beside the house there was a higher lookout reached by stone steps. Before the surrounding trees had grown up, that would have been an ideal place to watch the sea. I was like the children, I loved the little house, I could easily imagine the fire lit, the smoke curling up the little chimney the door barricaded against the storm and the two watchers happily puffing at their pipes sharing a yarn or two, while waiting for the pilchards to come into the bay, or checking the sailing ships coming up past the Dodman.

Looking at the construction of the place I wondered if it had also been used as a look out for the Spanish Armada beating its way up channel, not aware that Sir Francis Drake was waiting and watching for them on Plymouth Hoe, but only after he had finished that famous game of bowls.

Did he really say 'I will finish the game, and beat the Spanish after.' I like to believe that he did, he was a wily old sea dog, and he knew that the wind was against them; if you go onto Plymouth hoe and look up at his statue you see a sturdy, confident man, still gazing out across Plymouth sound ready to do battle.

When we had finally exhausted the endless questions and eaten our picnic all crammed in the little house we would finally end up at the cross . Built of Cornish granite on the very edge of the point, and 373 feet above the sea it stands proudly exposed to the elements on all sides, a powerful symbol of one man's love of God and nature. It has been used as a navigation aid for centuries but it is also a perfect spot for a picnic. Having walked out along the lane and across the top fields, the cross stands as a beacon, sending a message of peace. Sitting on the steps below the cross, munching a pasty, while gazing out into the bay towards Falmouth, or up along the coast to Fowey and Plymouth, is one of life's great pleasures. It was built in 1896 by the then vicar of Caerhayes the Rev George Martin, who loved the Dodman and who would often spend the night out there, and surely he would have spent it in our little house. The inscription on the cross reads

'In the firm hope of the second coming of our Lord Jesus Christ and for the

encouragement of those who serve Him. This cross is erected A.D.1896.

The Dodman is also the site of an Iron Age Hill Fort, the perfect location for a secure enclosure, close to the sea, for fishing, yet built on excellent productive soil, these ancient Celts were wise farmers and hunters.

We always walked back along the cliff path looking down at the sea hoping for the glimpse of a seal, or even a pod of dolphins swimming in the sparkling waters below. Sometimes, if we had stayed too long at the cross, a sea mist would start to roll in, and as we made our way back along the path, I was always reminded of those other souls who had lived and walked the same paths. I would visualize those ancient people tending their animals, digging in the earth for stones to make tools, and building their huts high on the

Dodman, secure in the knowledge that they had earthen ramparts all around them, shielding them from any unexpected attacks.

I could see them clad in skins, making their way down the stony cliffs to stand on the great flat rocks and catch fish to take back, and cook over the smoky fires, the family clustered around, and the east wind whistling in through the stone doorway. I longed to see just one of them, clad in skins hurrying along the path in front of us, just for a second, but there was only the sound of the wind and the waves below.

The gathering mist wrapped its arms around, holding us ransom in an eerie grey fog and shutting out the sight of the sea. I felt their elusive spirits all around us and was thankful that soon we would reach the stile and turn back along the side of the hill fort and into the sheltered lane leading back to Penare. The children would be asking what was for tea, and Toby would be charging ahead after a startled rabbit, and my ghosts would be lost in the mists of time as we headed home.

This was our Dodman, and when we heard that the Navy planned to create not only a firing range in our bay, but also to put spotters positioned on the Dodman, the locals were up in arms, here we go again, I thought , another campaign, a bit different than the last one, this time we had the might of the Royal Navy and the government against us.

Rob is typical of some Cornish folk and some men I guess, he hates confrontation, anything for an easy life, 'this will really effect the fishermen' he said, 'leave it to them.'

The fisherman are a strong band of men and I could see where he was coming from, this was man's work, leave well alone. Then my friend Jan rang me to say she was having a meeting with Jayne whose husband Nick was a fulltime fisherman, they wanted all the support that they could get. That was it I was hooked, pardon the pun, I realized that not only would the bay be affected and the fishing ruined, but with spotters on the hallowed Dodman we could even be barred from going out there with it eventually becoming M.O.D. property.

This was not on, so I joined the fight

This time I had a vague idea of what to expect, I certainly was not going to sign up for any five mile walks, but I would write letters, sign petitions and do the odd jumble sale. As usual the best laid plans went up in smoke, the campaign took off, I even got Rob involved, we petitioned the entire coastline communities. Rob and I ended up at St Mawes Sailing Club one sunny morning hoping to enlist their support in our fight. I was not sure about this, I knew that St Mawes was very up market, plus I guessed that there would be quite a few ex naval officers in the club.

So it was with some trepidation that we parked our old car outside and ventured in. The guys could not have been more supportive, and listening to them I realized that the Dodman is used as not only for navigation, but that it also holds a special place in the hearts of those who take to the sea. They would write letters to the minister, they would support the fishermen, they were definitely on our side, we left St Mawes feeling hopeful, it seemed that support was growing.

The following evening I found myself in Mevagissey Social Club, surrounded by real fishermen, not the Gorran Haven part timers I was used to. No these were the real thing, huge beards, pints in hand, men of few words, they listened to Jan and I as we said our piece, we needed them on our side. I felt pleased that my grandfather Edwin had been a Mevagissey fisherman, though I only vaguely remember him, just as a gold pocket watch and a friendly knee. I felt at home, there was a connection and once I knew that they would be with us, all guns blazing,. the fight was on.

CHAPTER FOURTEEN

A CREAM TEA

Because the National Trust owns the Dodman Point they became heavily involved in the campaign receiving letters from all over the country, the local representative Giles Clotworthy, told the media,

'We have never received such a volume of correspondence on any subject.'

This was really encouraging news for us, support was coming from every quarter, the Dodman with its stone cross obviously meant a great deal to so many people. We wondered, did we stand a chance against the might of the establishment. An election was coming up. We lobbied the shadow defence minister who promised if they got in they would review the situation. It became almost surreal, here we were a group of middle aged ladies having meetings with top politicians , demonstrating outside County Hall, infiltrating coffee mornings in Truro where the actual defence minister had been welcomed by the party faithful, or so he thought, only to be tackled by some of our campaign members who felt so strongly they nearly came to blows.

We knew that we had to get more media coverage, our local radio stations were brilliant but we had to take the fight up to the big boys. Then our luck changed and a reporter from non other than, The Times, agreed to come down and do a piece.

We were ecstatic, it was agreed that some of us would be delegated to walk him out to the Dodman, while I would stay and prepare an amazing cream tea at our house. The idea was that once he had been replenished with a Cornish cream tea, he would be bound to be very sympathetic to our cause.

Also, we had Nick Tomlinson, our local full time fisherman who was joining us for 'the tea' and our hopes were riding high.

It was a beautiful sunny day which was certainly to our advantage. The Dodman was wearing her best clothes, the lanes leading out were dry and clean and bordered by wild flowers, with the occasional butterfly fluttering along in front of the walkers.

Once they got through the lane leading out to the first gate they took the narrow path leading out to the high fields which are part of the ancient hill fort, and which provide a spectacular view of the azure blue of the sea, with the long stretch of Vault beach below, and the whole of St Austell bay, reaching up as far as Fowey and Rame Head stretched out before them.

They passed by my little stone look out house, no time to explore that, the Dodman was calling and she did not fail them. The sea was calm, gently washing onto the rocks below.

In the bay, a Mevagissey fishing boat was laden, and making her way back to port, the hungry gulls whirling around her hoping for a quick meal. A yacht was slowly sailing up past the mighty headland, and there was a clutch of smaller boats taking advantage of the good weather and fishing just off the Dodman.

I was an idyllic scene, we all thanked our lucky stars, it could have been so different. I have walked out to the cross in a gale force wind, the rain coming down in sheets and the sea sending in great waves which crashed onto the rocks below us sending the spray almost as high as the Dodman itself.

Back at home I had been busy baking tasty scones and making a huge Victoria sponge, having tried too hard with the first one which refused to rise sufficiently I calmed down and used my old recipe which worked like a dream. The sponge did what it was told and sat on one of my best plates filled with homemade jam and lightly dusted with icing sugar.

Rob had watched all this manic preparation with amusement, and was even more entertained when I got out my mother's best embroidered table cloth, decorated with a wonderful array of flowers. We were going to have china cups and saucers, not a mug in sight, we would show The Times, that we knew how to do things down here in Cornwall.

Rob had to go to work leaving me to try and be 'the hostess with the mostest'

I must admit I was anxious, I loved cooking and entertaining, but this was something different, so much was hanging on getting the right papers to take up our cause.

I need not have worried, they all arrived back in great spirits.

Nick, our tame fisherman was brilliant, very coherent and calm he stated his case clearly.

Full up with jam and cream, we were impressed, and so was the reporter, he went back to London, and we got the headlines.

The other big papers took up the story, we were on a roll.

Then we heard that the fisherman were going to make a big demonstration with fishing boats from all over the south coast joining in, this would have a huge impact on the situation. We were to demonstrate on the quay and the boats would assemble in Mevagissey harbour, we contacted all the organizations who were involved and waited with baited breath.

Some people were pessimistic, 'the fishermen won't come, they won't give up a day of fishing for some demonstration.'

I was not sure, I knew that the Mevagissey men would be there, but what about all the others, from all along the coast, they would be affected as well.

The fishing fraternity are not easy to assess, generally a law unto themselves, independent to a man, would they comply and turn up.

We waited on the quay, we had a good turn out, but it was the fishermen who we needed, quite a few of the Mevagissey boats were already there, some with placards and flags flying. It was beginning to look good, then someone shouted,

'Look what's coming,' and there they were, steaming towards the harbour, trawlers from all along the coast with banners reading,

'Fishing not Firing'

M.O.D. Miss the Point Cornwall Says NO.'

There were trawlers from Fowey, Falmouth, Padstow, plus a flotilla of smaller boats from all along the coast. It made the nationals, Colin Williams, from Mevagissey was quoted in The Guardian saying 'Democracy has gone out of the window. We have got a whole generation of civil servants in Whitehall who just don't listen to people any more.'

It warmed the heart, the sight of the large gathering of people on the quayside all from different backgrounds, and not your usual type of agitators, yet there they were standing up for what they believed, and the land and sea that they were passionate about.

Then to crown it all, the boats, all different shapes and sizes and finally the big trawlers, what a picture they made. Pictures which quickly appeared in all the newspapers, and on the television.

The M.O.D. were not beaten yet, they still intended to begin firing and a date was set.

Having been brought up in Plymouth, and with a father who had been a serving naval officer I was torn, but I was convinced that on this occasion they had got it wrong, and with a grandfather who had been a fisherman I knew where my loyalties lay.

The day of the firing Rob and I walked out to the Dodman, it was a fine day with excellent visibility, a crowd had assembled. Everyone was waiting to see what would happen. We sat on the steps of the old stone cross and gazed out to sea. A number of small boats were fishing in the bay below us, prime fishing grounds for the smaller craft.

Then a some of the bigger boats began appearing, but they looked tiny against the imposing outline of the naval frigate based further out in the bay and preparing to commence firing at the marker buoys already in position.

Someone beside us began to laugh.

'You know what it is,' he exclaimed, 'Trelawney's Navy.'

The boats had positioned themselves directly in the line of fire.

We were told later that the fishermen were requested to move out of the way, but they carried on fishing. On the cliff top we could see what was happening, there was an air of exuberance, the Cornish boys were not going to be told where they could or could not fish, they stayed put.

The Navy made repeated requests over the radio, all to no avail, eventually they gave up.

Lieutenant Commander Steve Kenny commented after the exercise:

'We have been firing at Portland for over thirty years and we have worked out a mutual understanding with the fishermen. Nine times out of ten we were able to accommodate them each other.

That is something we have not been able to work out with the Cornish fishermen.'

Reading these comments in the paper later I could not suppress a smile, the Navy had obviously underestimated the strength of the

Cornish character.

They later accused the fishermen of mounting an organized protest but arriving back in Mevagissey harbour they all maintained that they had been going about their lawful business in the rich fishing grounds of Dodman point.

When interviewed Les Hunkin, whose son John was skipper of the fishing boat, The Heather Ann, admitted that his boat was deliberately getting in the line of fire, but he added that other boats, which were mainly scallopers from Falmouth and Looe had been there for a fortnight, yet the Navy had put their marker buoys right in the middle of the trawl ground.

He explained that it was one of the main trawling ground for scallops and white fish, such as sole. This was due to the fact that the bottom of the sea, off the Dodman, is sandy, and said that any shells fired would create havoc and ruin the callipers gear.

We all walked back along the coastal path in high spirits, Trelawney's Navy had won the day. I felt a great sense of pride, that independent spirit which had always been part of the Cornish fishing community was still alive and well. It took a lot to rile them, but like a sleeping tiger, and Trelawney's Army, of long ago, once woken they bowed to no man.

Eventually there was a kind of compromise, the plan to have part of the Dodman fenced off for spotters was shelved, instead, helicopters would be used to mark the shots.

The marker buoys would be moved farther out, the days of firing would be reduced, it was a triumph for people power. What I found heartening was the way so many people all coming from different perspectives had banded together in their love of Cornwall and that very special place, Dodman Point.

CHAPTER FIFTEEN

THE WRECK OF THE KATIE CLUETT

Though we had fought to preserve the Dodman we were well that it had two faces, one benign and peaceful, the other cruel and wild. Walking to the Dodman while enjoying the different flowers appearing in the hedges, and stopping to admire endless views, is a totally different experience from the image you perceive when you are out in the bay.

The bay between Gorran Haven and the Dodman is fringed by the long sweep of Vault beach, forget Bondi beach, Vault provides a mile of golden sand and the sea is always crystal clear. The great arm of the Dodman seems to almost curve around Vault, sheltering it from some of the worse weather. Access to this isolated spot is limited. There is the cliff path from Gorran Haven, or for brave motorists, a narrow lane which leads to the National Trust car park at the top of the cliff.

The walk, through fields, down the narrow winding path to the beach below, provides the walker with the opportunity to take in the magnificent views, and look down at any swimmers as they enjoy the sparkling, crystal clear waters. Anyone lucky enough to have a boat can land on Vault, but it can be deceptive, the odd freak roller can cause havoc, but the reward is worth the effort.

It is the perfect beach for those who want to get away from it all. When we land on Vault I always feel that it is the nearest thing to landing on a desert island, there are no cafes, no beach shops, nothing but a huge expanse of the sand and the odd figure in the distance.

This means of course that travelling with supplies is essential especially plenty of drinks because it can get very hot, but all this is part of its charm.

A trip to Vault by sea would sometimes include a circular tour out around the Dodman, and the twins would always demand that Rob tell some stories of the different wrecks which the mighty headland had claimed over the years. Even on a calm summer day, when our little boat was positioned directly under the headland, there was always the feeling of menace. The huge rocks which lie at the bottom, act as a warning, and the current is always strong, you know that in an easterly gale you could be washed onto those massive rocks and smashed to bits.

What hope would any ship wrecked sailor have. Rob would tell of some who had managed to scramble onto the rocks and climb the towering cliffs, but looking up at the cross from the sea we would all wonder how anyone could survive being wrecked on the Dodman and then managing to scale the treacherous cliffs above

There was always the feeling of dicing with danger when our small boat circled around those huge boulders.

Then, then a friendly seal would suddenly pop his head up and we would forget wrecked ships and concentrate on the soulful eyes of the grey seal, curiously gazing at us, before diving back down into the safety of his own environment below.

Looking up at the cross and out across the bay on a warm spring day when the primroses have begun to shyly immerge from the dark earth, and the fishing boats are gently steaming out to the grounds; it seems almost impossible to realize that the Dodman has a history of death. In the days of sail and before the navigational aids, we now have, the mighty Dodman stood as a beacon to all sailors coming up the channel

. In good weather it was a welcome sight, nearly home, but in a wild dark sea with driving rain and an easterly gale blowing it became a deathly hazard.

One ship which met her fate on the mighty Dodman was the Katie Cluett, a three masted schooner of 130 tons and built at Fowey. She was famous for her speed and graceful lines, but not only was she fast, she was a pretty ship, with graceful lines.

I could easily imagine her speeding across the bay, her sails billowing in the south-east wind, as she set off from Cornwall on her way to the rough seas of Newfoundland where she was involved in the salt fish trade

She belonged to Captain Alfred Prettyman who lived in the tiny village of Pentewan, and where his descendants still live to this day.

In 1917, the Katie Cluett was in a convoy returning from St Brieuc in France, it was Christmas Eve, and Captain Alfred Prettyman had a wife and small daughter eagerly awaiting his return back home in Pentewan. There was a strong East South East wind blowing, and it was dark, and the sea was rough and visibility was poor. The Captain could have put into Falmouth and waited until day light to make the final leg of the journey, but I imagine because it was Christmas Eve he and his crew were anxious to get back home he decided to sail through the night.

It was some time after midnight when that fastest and most graceful ship ran ashore onto the killer rocks of the Dodman. Somehow, three members of her crew managed to get ashore and despite the darkness, and now gale force winds, they clambered up the cliff where a Gorran Haven fisherman, Bob Ball was quietly dozing in the little stone look out house.

He was rudely awakened by the mate from the Katie Cluett hammering on the door for help. Bob immediately called out the coast guard and the Mevagissey lifeboat, but neither could help because of such horrendous conditions.

Captain Alfred Prettyman's body could not be found when the coast guards began searching at first light. Then one of the crew seemed to think that he had seen him heading back to the ship, but in the darkness, he could not be sure. Eventually, two days later, he was found, by a Gorran Haven fisherman at low tide, caught in between the deadly rocks at the foot of the Dodman. The villagers later found children's toys, bought as Christmas presents, washed up on the shore line, a pathetic reminder of the wife and small daughter, who had waited in vain, at home in Pentewan, for his return.

There were other ships and fishing boats who had been lost on the Dodman, all of them tragedies, but the story of the Katie Cluett strikes a special chord, because of the time, Christmas Eve and because of the family waiting, and because somehow in your heart you expect Christmas to be a time of joy, but the sea has no respect for such emotion.

I always remember the Soloman Browne the Penlee life boat from Mousehole, lost on the 19th of December 1981 while going to the rescue of a tanker the Union Star. All the crew of the life boat and the tanker were lost that night, when the news hit Cornwall the next morning the entire county was devastated. Bad enough to lose the tanker and all her crew, but to lose the brave life boat crew who had gone to sea that terrible night to answer the call for help, was a double tragedy.

Such is the character of the sea and this is understood by all those in the coastal communities. The sea is a beguiling mistress, beautiful in repose, yet cruel and unforgiving when roused showing no mercy for those who are caught in her icy depths.

Mousehole is famous for its Christmas lights, all the boats in the harbour are beautifully decorated and lit up, as well as the harbour itself.

Thousands flock to the little village, but it will never forget it's brave lifeboat men, every year on the anniversary of that terrible night the Christmas lights are switched off for an hour in remembrance of those bravest souls who perished while going to the aid of others in the sea.

CHAPTER SIXTEEN

HEMMICK DAYS

So the Dodman was saved and we all heaved a sigh if relief, and the walks out to the cross could continue and the little house could still be explored happily by all the other generations of children who would go through the old gate and climb the stone look out . Often once the twins were older we would make a day of it and having eaten our picnic sitting on the steps of the cross and gazing out across the bay down to the Gull Rock and Falmouth; we would follow the coast path along and down to our favourite beach, Hemmick. Hemmick hold a special place in our hearts

Rob's father was born in the small cottage which stands near the entrance to the beach. The family had lived there for over a hundred years, with no mains water or electricity, raising six children in two bedrooms. Walking along the path from the Dodman, and looking down at the first sight of Hemmick always lifts the heart. This is a real Cornish cove, with a stretch of golden sand divided by the rock formation into different areas, thus providing the illusion of owning your own patch of beach for the day. I always feel that making the effort to go to Hemmick is like having a mini holiday. There are no facilities, it's just you and the beach, so planning is all important, but the feeling of peace always prevails, cut off from the hustle and bustle of Gorran Haven, and reached only by a one track, winding lane Hemmick stands alone, a unique Cornish cove.

The family cottage is now a holiday home, initially, something Rob found very hard to cope with, when they were growing up, and both Vicky and Michael had expressed their desire to 'live in the cottage at Hemmick.' When we found out that it was to become a holiday let, we all said, 'not another holiday home, not Hemmick,' but Vicky very sensibly thought of it another way.

'Surely,' she commented, 'you could say that having it as a holiday let means that lots of other families can enjoy the chance to live in the cottage by the beach, if only for a week.'

She definitely had a point, but it is still hard to see strangers coming out of the old gate when for so many years it was the family home. Rob's grandfather was a postman, having lost his hand in a mangle cutting machine, and having six children to support he became employed by the Royal Mail, delivering the letters on his bike. After he died, the old bike was hung on the wall in the dairy, a memento to all the years spent peddling around the parish in all winds and weathers. As a child Rob can remember being fascinated by it, with huge wide handle bars, and tyres as thick as some motor bikes, and a wire basket on the front to carry the post. It had no brakes and was heavy as lead, yet he pedaled and pushed this antique machine all around the parish and out lying hamlets with only one working hand and a metal hook to control it. Men were made of strong stuff back then, no disability benefits, they just had to get on with it.

Hemmick is situated at the very bottom of the cove reached by steep hills on both sides, so he had to navigate the bike up to the top of the hill before he could even start. All this with an iron hook where he had lost his hand, he must have been the tough.

Rob's grandmother was no less tough, giving birth to six children, plus milking the couple of cows they kept and fetching all their drinking water from a pipe in the cliff. Any other water came from the stream which ran down the valley and onto the beach. The nearest neighbour was at least half a mile away at the top of the hill so she had to be totally independent. Add to all this, making butter and collecting the eggs which she then loaded into a large basket and would set off to walk up the hill to Penare where she would collect more produce to carry all the way into Mevagissey to sell. Times were hard, no doubt, but she lived well into her nineties and saw mains water and electricity come to the cottage.

It was a family of boys with just one girl, and even when grown men and with families of their own and living around the parish, every Sunday morning they would all come back to Hemmick. The official reason was so that the grandchildren could visit, but Sunday mornings always included a game of cricket in one of the meadows beside the cottage. Though isolated and basic there must have been a certain kind of magic which the location provided, plus the companionship for five boys all close in age, with a madness for cricket and fishing. In the winter they had the entire beach to themselves, they all knew the best rocks to catch a bass or a mackerel, no wonder they kept returning and it always held a special place in all their hearts.

The magic of the place will not appeal to everyone, too isolated, no ice creams, no toilet, terrible access, but to those of us who still have a touch of the pioneering spirit, it is bliss.

We first took the twins to Hemmick when they were six months old, after all the nappies and sleepless nights I desperately needed a Hemmick day. The sun was shining, the beach washed clean by the winter storms, was a clear stretch of sand. We were lucky to get a parking spot at the entrance to the beach and unloaded the twin pram and proceeded to haul it along the sand.

It was July, the sea was inviting and we had a small rubber dingy. We loaded the twins into the dingy and with Rob one side and me the other we just floated in the balmy sea. Vicky and Michael loved it and I think that their first introduction to Hemmick had a lasting effect on them as it has to many others, when the sun shines, 'Hemmick calls.'

The sun doesn't always shine on Hemmick, it would be a lie to say that it does, we have sat there with dark clouds hanging heavily above us, straining our eyes for enough blue sky to make a sailor a pair of trousers or even a handkerchief. We have huddled into a tiny tent wrapped in towels, while the Cornish rain cascaded down eventually finding its way into the tent and down our backs. But we have also spent magical evenings cooking sausages on a barbeque, swimming in a soft velvety sea in the moonlight and singing around a bonfire on the beach, frightening the owners of a yacht who had dropped anchor in what they thought was a quiet cove, to find that it was alive with a crowd of very merry locals. Happy memories, Hemmick memories and hopefully many more to come.

CHAPTER SEVENTEEN

THE CRICKET FETE

You cannot beat a real summer day in Cornwall, which is why so many visitors keep returning. The scenery of course is unique, and the choice of scenery spectacular, from our softer south coast to the rugged wildness of the north. Having survived the winter storms and the promise of spring, when the summer finally arrives we put the winter days behind us and quickly get into summer mode regardless. The annual cricket fete is always held in August, and the main requirement for success, is a sunny day.

Having been born in Plymouth I had no idea what a fete was, and I watched with great interest the preparations which preceded this event.

'How does it work,' I asked Rob.

'We have different stalls and cream teas, do you fancy running a stall?'

I thought about it, 'Well I could do, but most stalls and competitions have already been planned.'

'We could do with something different ,' Rob commented, and that was it, the opportunity to let my imagination run wild, what could I do?

Then I remembered something I had seen on T.V. a village fete with, wait for it, a fortune teller, ideal I thought .

Without telling Rob I made a few plans, sorting out the outfit which consisted of a long black skirt and shawl, a brilliant black wig and glasses. Looking in the mirror I was impressed, all I needed was a basket of pegs.

I tried it out on Rob one afternoon when he got back from work, suddenly appearing in the kitchen when he opened the door, 'what the hell,' he was certainly surprised, and the fact that he had to hold onto the work top was most encouraging.

'Cross my palm with silver sir,' he was speechless, Vicky and Michael hiding in the hall, were helpless with laughter.

'Well what do you think?'

Never one for effusive bursts of praise all I got was, 'Yes, it's alright.'

'Yes but do you think the cricket club will like the idea?' I persisted.

He was non committal, but I was on a roll.

'I'm going to try it on Jane,' I said.

I found a wicker basket, loaded it up with pegs and made my way to Jane's house. When she opened the door her face was a picture, coming from Derby and not used to gypsies, knocking on her front door, she was totally unprepared for the sight before her.

'Buy a peg Missus, have your fortune told?'

Jane held onto the door and began to back away for me.

'No thank you,' she spluttered, 'not today.'

'Jane it's me,' she was still closing the door, 'it's me,' I managed to say beginning to laugh.

It took her a few seconds to register the fact, so I whipped off the wig and then she began to laugh too.

'It's for the cricket fete,' I informed her, 'I'm going to tell some fortunes, what do you think?'

'You had me fooled,' was her reply, 'come in a minute I have something that might be helpful.'

She produced a pack of tarot cards, 'you could use these to tell some fortunes.'

I marched home delighted, she had obviously been fooled and the pack of cards would be a great help. I had been planning a crystal ball, but the cards would be a welcome addition. However, I had no idea exactly what tarot cards were, I looked at them briefly and then moved on to organizing the rest of my act.

I shall need the tent put up,' I informed Rob, 'and what I really would like is to ride into the cricket field on a horse.'

'You need to ask Ronald,' was the reply.

Ronald, Rob's brother agreed to my plan, I was welcome to make an entrance by riding their huge horse into the cricket field in all my gypsy regalia.

I used a glass crab pot marker wrapped in a silk scarf for a crystal ball, I had Jane's tarot cards and I was set.

The day of the fete dawned, it was ideal weather, the tent was positioned on the field with a small table and chairs inside, and a homemade notice proclaiming:

THE WORLD FAMOUS MADAM ZARRA FORTUNE TELLER

Outside the cricket field I was dressed, and ready for my big entrance.

Ronald helped me up on to the horse and we set off. I had forgotten just how high it is on top of a large horse, I knew that it would ruin the entire effect if I fell off, so I held on for grim death, and attempted to be a regal Madam Zarra.

I was quite pleased to dismount when we reached the tent and I was somewhat surprised to find that there was quite a queue waiting to have their fortunes told.

I adopted a French accent and set to work, it was quite disconcerting to realize that my disguise was so good, people who I knew, and who should have known me, were taking the whole thing very seriously. The cards were perfect I spread them out and after reading the palms, I concocted various stories which I matched with the pictures as I went along.

What I had not bargained for was the death card, but I quickly whipped that one out of the pack saying, 'you haven't been very well but good health is on the horizon.'

Because I knew so many of the people coming into the tent, I became adept at matching my predictions to their circumstances, one lady in particular turned over a card which conveyed good fortune. Holding her hand and gazing into her eyes I said, 'I can see wealth coming your way.'

She tightened her grip on mine, 'are you sure?' she whispered.

 'Yes, it may be a while, but it will happen.'

She went out of the tent with a smile on her face, nothing to this fortune telling lark I thought, just be positive and keep the people happy.

The afternoon was a great success, and once I came out of character I forgot all about it, that is until I found that some of 'my predictions' were actually coming true.

'That fortune teller was good,' I heard people saying, 'are you going to get her again next year?'

I kept quiet, then the lady for whom I had predicted good fortune suddenly began driving around the village in a brand new car. It was quite disconcerting, did I have a gift, could I give Paul Daniels a run for his money.

Rob ever the realist, thought the whole thing hilarious, 'the only gift you have is spinning a great tale,' he said, 'drama queen to the last.'

Madam Zarra was such a success that I resurrected her just one more time, the following year. We concocted a tiny caravan from a friend's trailer, unfortunately it was not ideal fortune telling weather. The mist rolled in across the cricket field, the rain poured down and as I peered across to the pavilion I decided that Madam Zarra would not be appearing at Gorran Cricket Fete again.

'No worries' said the committee, 'we need someone to man the, white elephant stall, it always makes money.'

So, I became an instant expert on antiques finding that people will chuck out an amazing assortment of articles which others will discover they have been waiting for all their lives. The first, white elephant stall, proved to be a steep learning curve.

My mother had left me some dinner plates which I had never liked, very plain with a green and yellow stripe around the edge. I decided that I would donate these plates to the stall, thus raising a bit of money for the fete and making room in my cupboards for some new plates from Woolworth's. I stacked the plates neatly on my stall, put a price tag of two pounds fifty on them and was amazed when a friend grabbed my arm.

'Are these for sale?'

'Oh yes, do you want them?' I asked.

She looked surprised, 'do you know what they are, they are Clarice Cliff.'

I had to admit that this meant nothing at all to me, all I knew was that I had never liked the set, and much preferred my new blue and white ones.

I just wanted to get rid of them, and she went off with a genuine bargain that day. Later, when various antique programmes began appearing on T.V. I realized that I could have made a handsome profit that day.

It still did not alter the fact that I genuinely did not like them.

There is something about a white elephant stall at a village fete on a summer day.

I found that summer visitors are suckers for a bargain, and to be fair many of the items on display were bargains, but many, were definitely not. Still they sold, old pieces of pottery which I now described, as 'possibly early Clarice Cliff,' were snapped up, old paintings which I attributed to 'early Renoir,' he spent many holidays in Cornwall,' were also sold.

People chucked out old wet suits, summer dresses which had seen better days, canoes, prams, children's toys all made their way to my stall. I erected a clothes rail and put the prettiest dresses at the front of the rail, selling them to anyone who expressed an interest, regardless of the fact that I was selling a size eight to a size sixteen customer.

The sun was shining, the cream teas were nearly sold out, and I would always knock down prices for those who I knew really needed it, the others were fair game.

One lady always made a bee line to my stall.

She lived locally, in a small barn tucked away in the parish. The only time I ever saw her was at the cricket fete which in a village, is unusual to say the least.

Most people surface at some events throughout the year, but not this lady. Her only mode of transport was a battered old bike which she would park up against the wall of the pavilion while she rummaged through my white elephant stall.

She never brought dresses or paintings, it was the essentials of everyday living which she required. Old plates, a nearly new saucepan, a decent radio, a hair dryer, she piled it all beside her old bike and sat quietly having a cup of tea before making the home ward journey.

When the initial rush of the afternoon was over and I was packing up, she wandered across. There was an electric heater placed at the side of the stall, something which had not sold, considering that it had been a very hot sunny afternoon, and people's minds were not on electric heaters.

The price I had hastily marked on it was three pounds, probably one of the most expensive items on the entire stall.

She produced her tattered old purse and I could see that she was counting out how much she had left.

'I'm reducing everything,' I said quickly, she looked up.

'It would really be useful in the barn, but I shall have to take the rest home and come back for it.' She hesitated, 'that's if I can afford it.'

I did not want to offend her, 'it's yours for one fifty,' I said, 'and I'll throw in the clothes dryer if it's any use.'

Her face lit up, and she handed me the money.

'I tell you what,' I said, 'I'm packing up now, if you hang on I will give you a lift home with all your stuff then you can come back and just ride your bike back.'

We loaded all her shopping in the boot of the car and set off. When I helped her to carry the odd assortment of items to her so called front door, I was amazed. It was almost totally obscured by masses of ivy reaching from the top of the old barn to the ground, there must have been a window somewhere but I could see no sign of it. She made no attempt to open the door, but turned to thank me, it was clear she did not want any more contact.

That was that, she continued to appear for a few more years and then I never saw her again. I would never discover what had happened to her, she had obviously left the area, nobody seemed to know, one of Cornwall's many mysteries.

CHAPTER EIGHTEEN

CORNISH CELEBRATIONS

Though we had left Church Park and moved to Gorran Haven I found that I sometimes suffered with withdrawals for Mevagissey. I missed my afternoon walks when the twins were in the double pram and I could push them down to Hitler's Walk and gaze down on my mother's village

Mevagissey Feast was always a great excuse to go back, the Feast of St Peter went way back in time. I remember my mother and aunts fondly reminiscing about Feast.

I was always fascinated hearing about the number of different chapels in one small village, each one celebrating with their own chapel teas and singing.

The old photos show crowds of happy people all dressed in their best, lining the narrow streets. How did they all manage to look so smart?

No washing machines, having to fetch water from the village pump, heating the heavy irons on the old Cornish range and cooking for families of eight to ten.

Yet there they are, most of the ladies wearing starched white blouses, topped with wonderful picture hats. The children all beautifully turned out with white pinafores worn over their dresses, long hair neatly braided.

The fishermen, not to be outdone by the ladies, in white shirts and waistcoats, and sporting bowler hats.

The old photographs are testament to the values of tradition and community, something which still plays a vital role in Cornish life.

Time moves on, and now we have a fish festival on the quay, with local fish being cooked by various chefs, all offering mouth watering dishes.

There is an amazing firework display on the final evening, which we all say easily equals any display anywhere.

Sitting on the grass up at Hitler's Walk, looking down on the village and quay, with the lights of the cottages twinkling in the darkness, and the outline of the fishing boats lit up by the endless rockets bursting above our heads, is simply quite magical.

The old ways are not forgotten, there is still a fishing boat race, the boats all steaming across the bay flags flying in the breeze, the supporters lined up along the quay, this is generally followed by a homemade raft race, with bags of flour being chucked at opposing teams, rafts sinking, and the crew ending up in the water.

There is a fete and fair on the football field, and the chapels still hold their teas, and the Flora is still danced through the streets, the sound of the drum calling to the dancers as they weave their way along.

Music and singing is a big part of the celebrations, Mevagissey Male Voice Choir always gives a concert as does The Ladies Choir. I was lucky enough to be invited to join the ladies and it always gives me a thrill to be part of such and ancient celebration. Its a celebration of tradition and community and having lived in Cornwall for many years and coming from a city life, I have realized the importance of preserving that way of life for future generations.

Visitors to Cornwall love the various celebrations, crab catching competitions are very popular. I have seen professional city traders down on their hands and knees with their children, the crab line dangling in the water, immersed in the excitement of catching a small crab.

This is the dream, the simple life, the old traditions which draw people together being part of something bigger than all of us the sense of belonging

Back in Gorran Haven the old traditions still thrive, one has been resurrected and heralds the beginning of the summer .Easter is the time for eggs and, The Great Egg Rolling Competition, was started a few years ago

Would anyone come, would modern children want to spend time decorating boiled eggs and then having them judged for small prizes, before rolling them down Church street to find a winner

Well, the answer was a resounding 'yes'.

What started as a small 'shall we try it' idea has grown. Easter heralds a new dawn, visitors rush down to Cornwall, the lights go on in the cottages and suddenly the heart of the village comes alive again. The egg rolling commences at the tiny church of St Just looking out over the harbour, the eggs are judged and then they are rolled down the hill to the beach. The tiny hill is crowded with families and children all clutching their carefully decorated eggs. The judging is done inside the church, it used to be outside in the courtyard, but the numbers have grown so much that the eggs are lined up inside the church, while the anxious parents and children all peer in through the door hoping for a prize.

When the judging has been completed the eggs are returned to their owners and the rolling commences, all sorted into different classes.

Little ones are lifted onto shoulders to watch the fun. Wind, rain, hail even, people still turn out, occasionally we have been treated to some sun, but regardless of the weather conditions everyone turns out visitors, and locals alike. The eggs roll down the hill some crash at the bottom, others survive and are retrieved by tiny hands to be taken home and cherished. When the egg rolling is completed, everyone climbs up the cliff path to the 'Memorial Village Hall', nestled in the side of the cliff and boasting fabulous views across the beach to Little Perhaver for the prize giving and hot soup.

People love it, 'when are you having the egg rolling?' is one of the first questions asked.

It is the same for the New Year's Day swim, started a few years ago to raise money for charity by a friend Nona, the idea just took off. The beach can be windy, the sea rough, the rain bucketing down, but the swim goes on, hardy locals and visitors who have only come for the Christmas holiday they all jump into the freezing water and come out beaming, it has become a tradition. Then back again to the village hall and the obligatory raffle, a vital part of any village celebration.

While Mevagissey has its 'Feast' Gorran Haven has Gala Day. Because the village is clustered around the beach and because the beach is at the heart of village life it seemed appropriate to celebrate around the quay and the harbour. Run by the fishermen's society, everyone joins in, with boat and swimming races, cream teas, visits from the rescue services, helicopters displays, and if we are lucky, the Fowey life boat.

Naturally all this takes a great deal of organization, getting the tide right is the number one priority, out for the morning for the rowing and swimming races, then in for the greasy pole event, in the afternoon. Having been very involved with the cricket fete I managed to avoid taking on a role, and just enjoyed the day. The beach is always packed, children are lining up for various races, the small boats are being rowed blindfold, and the bigger boats are revving up for the fixed throttle races and everyone is busy registering for the final event of the day, the greasy pole.

This solid piece of equipment, a huge pole placed on the edge of the quay is anchored down and the object of the exercise is to give the participants a pillow each, send them out over the water on the pole {which has been liberally dosed with washing up liquid} and then let battle commence. The first one who falls off the pole into the water is the loser, while the winner then lives on to fight another day.

'Would you run the greasy pole,' I was asked a few years ago, and remembering what fun it is to watch it I foolishly said, 'yes.'
This meant that I was given a Harbour Gala tea shirt and immediately became an official.
'You will help, won't you?' I asked Rob. Previously he had been doing rescue boat, and I think that had appealed more to his idea of a good time, but with a bit of gentle persuasion, he finally agreed.
'I don't know what all the fuss is about,' I said merrily, 'It will be fun.'

The Gala Day dawned and everything went with a swing, someone handed me a clip board and pen, and I realized that there were endless lists of names on various pieces of paper. All the different classes, all the different ages, including adults both men and women. 'We better get out onto the end of the quay,' I shouted to Rob trying to make myself heard above all the fun. The I looked out at the quay, it was crowded with people all waiting to see the 'greasy pole' competition.

The quay is the perfect place for swimmers to jump off, one of the rites of passage living in Gorran Haven is to jump off the end of the quay. When the primary children up at Gorran School finish their last year, on the day they break up, they all rush down to the beach, and still in their school uniforms, all run along the quay to the end where like lemmings, they all jump off into the water.

Visitors sitting on the beach are amazed to see a line of school children all jumping fully dressed off the end of the quay.

The trouble with jumping off the quay is the fact that the fishing boats are all moored beside the end of the quay, and they all have to motor in past the jumpers. This can be worrying, boats do not have brakes, but nothing will stop this local past time, its the greatest fun and its tradition.

We have notices all over the quay, warning swimmers to be aware of the boats coming in to moor up and the local kids know exactly when to jump.

At least on Gala day there would be no boats coming in, so I knew that would not be a worry.

Looking at the huge list I had been given of those wanting to take part in the great greasy pole event, my heart sank. Seeing the pole hanging out over the quay had obviously inspired both children and adults alike, many of them visitors to the village. The local boys were well used to leaping off the quay without giving it a second thought and the greasy pole competition gave them that extra buzz of trying to knock each other off into the water below. I knew that it would be a slightly different situation for children who were new to the event. Jumping off the quay is one thing, sitting astride a slippery pole with a straw pillow in your hand trying to dodge being catapulted into the water below, while being watched by a huge crowd, is quite another.

Rob had organized the rescue boats and armed with a megaphone I asked for the youngest names on the list to come forward. Two local lads immediately sprung into action, they wriggled out onto the pole and Rob shouted 'go' and battle commenced. Their supporters were loud behind us egging them on and cheering. They were both hanging on for dear life and whacking each other for all they were worth, then the biggest one suddenly lost his balance and toppled down into the water with a resounding splash, quickly surfacing with a huge grin on his face and swimming to the steps. It proceeded until we got to the girls' section.

One little girl who shyly came forward hardly looked as though she was the required twelve years old plus the girl I had to put her against was quite a chunky young lady.

'Are you sure you want to do this?' I whispered in her ear.
She smiled up at me nodding, I looked at her mother just behind the barricade we had put up to keep the immediate area around the pole safe.

'She's fine,' she said. I was not at all sure about it, but the tiny girl was already out on the pole, pillow in her hand. Her opponent gingerly made her way out and they sat facing each other. If I was a betting person I would have put my cash on the chunky girl, but I would have lost my money.

'Go,' Rob shouted and the big one swung her pillow, the little one dodged and immediately retaliated with a huge swipe, the other girl wobbled and then fell off the pole down into the water below. I could hardly believe it. Then rather than edge back onto the quay she gracefully let go and slide down into the water as well. The crowd roared their appreciation for the tiny winner who then took on all the rest of the twelve year old girls, finally easily winning her class.

Some of the watchers seeing what was required of them, decided to pull out of the competition, while the older boys loved every moment, desperate to do battle with their best pals.

The dads, were another section who bristled with optimistic enthusiasm. Looking at some of them I was pleased that the greasy pole was solid and well anchored. Dads bursting out of tight wet suits clamoured to be put against their best mates, eager to show off to their watching families. Once on the pole, I noticed that it had an instant calming effect, the male ego rapidly subsided as they realized that balancing was a top priority, whacking your opponent came way down the list.

Down they went into the water, coming up with huge smiles on their faces, posing for photos to show when they got home.

The bigger they are, the harder they fall.

By this time the excitement had reached fever pitch, people were shouting, the quay was full to bursting and trying to run the whole event fairly was quite a challenge. We made it to the finals and low and behold, in the mixed final we ended up with a girl against one of the local boys.

The granddaughter of a local family she was down on holiday and had stayed on throughout the competition. I was concerned that she would not stand a chance against the stocky cocky lad, who slide out onto the pole encouraged by loud support from all his friends.

The girl was not wearing a wet suit, instead she just had on a flimsy bikini which worried me, would it stay on, or would she provide the watching crowd with more of a show that expected. The lad took a swipe, she shuddered under the impact, but hung on. He began showing off, waving a his pillow around before walloping her with all his strength. She hit back, but without the power that he had.

Her whacks just bounced off him, he was becoming very confident, laughing back at the crowd as he aimed another hit. That was his undoing, the girl saw her chance and aimed all her strength at him, taken by surprise, he was shaken from his perch and seizing the opportunity she followed it up with another resounding hit, sending him off the pole into the water below.

All the ladies on the quay cheered, it was a fantastic win for girl power, and I must admit, I was delighted, she well and truly deserved her medal that day.

I was relieved when the show was over, it was the final event of the day, all that was left was the prize giving and calling out the raffle winners. We had to stay out on the quay to supervise taking down the pole and stop the kids all keen to have another go on it. Finally it was all safe and we could make our way to the beach. The prize giving was going well, children flushed with success, went up to be presented with their medals from Ernest Oliver chairman of Gorran Haven Fisherman's Society. All the money was going towards the upkeep of the big cellars and the quay.

People were beginning to pack up for the day the beach was emptying.

We heaved a sigh of relief, it was our chance to have a swim and so we waded out into the balmy water and lazily swam out into the harbour turning to float and look back at the beach and the church, now shaded by the gathering shadows as the evening light faded. It had been another great Gala Day, the weather, all important had not let us down, a good time was had by one and all, nobody had drowned, and best of all the sun was still shining on the quay. Time to get some fish and chips, open a bottle of wine and relax.

CHAPTER NINETEEN

A SATURDAY MORNING

Saturday mornings are special, everyone seems to be out and about. You can have weekdays in the winter when you will only see the occasional hardy dog walker making their way down towards the wind swept beach and quay, but Saturdays are different, winter or summer the villager seems to come alive, people want to see each other, have a chat and catch up on the weeks news.

How many small villages have a real live bakery? As soon as you get to the top of Church street the unmistakable smell of freshly baked bread comes drifting up the street tickling the taste buds.

Walking down Church street you pass one of the original old bake houses, Zion cottage. This would have produced the same mouthwatering smells for hundreds of years, to tantalize the villagers waiting for their dinners to be cooked.

The tiny church of St Just or Chapel of Ease, stands near the bottom of the street, originally the site of a Celtic hermit's home, there has been a church there since the fifteenth century. It has be rebuilt many times, falling into disuse at one stage and in 1690 it was being used as a store for the fishermen to house their gear and nets. The services were then transferred to 'The Watch House' on the beach, previously used to detect any free traders, or as I prefer to think of them, smugglers.

The restoration was done in 1885 and the little church was back in business. More recently it was given a new lease of life and care by creating a memorial area at the side of the building where there are plaques to remember loved ones. These plaques have been greatly welcomed and I often think that to be remembered anywhere, a plaque beside the sea listening to the sounds of the waves is as good as it gets.

There is an alley beside the church which leads out to the sea and tucked away neatly in the corner is a small bench. There has always been a bench in this exact spot, just big enough for two to sit and beach watch. Visitors and locals who live in the cottages will often bring their coffee out onto the bench to sit and enjoy the boats steaming out into the bay, and watch the early morning swimmers heading out towards the Red Rock.

I love the little bench because of its position, generally sheltered, and also because of the inscription on it. It is dedicated to Prue, one of the daughters of Marjorie and John Fisher Williams who built the beautiful grey stone house which stands looking out over Vault beach and the bay. I have a book Prue's mother, Marjorie wrote about their years at Lamledra, in the book, which was written during the First World War there are photographs of Prudence and the descriptions of her somehow fit with the small bench dedicated to her memory.

There is a chapter in the book which describes Prue, as a small girl singing at the top of her voice, 'blue sea, blue sea,' upon arriving back in Cornwall, and running to kiss their old donkey in the field below the house.

I like to think of her coming down into the village and sitting in the same spot where her bench now stands. It has recently been replaced, the old one showing the signs of regular use, and hopefully, the new one, will last many more years; so the memory of a little girl in a white bonnet singing 'blue sea blue sea', will live on, and Prue's bench will continue to provide the perfect resting place to enjoy a sunny morning in Gorran Haven.

Turning into Rattle street the smell of pasties and bread leads you on. Cakebreads is a family business and has been part of village life as long as I can remember. It is run by Ralph and Barbara Noot. I often think that they represent the last example of the old village shop being at the heart of the community.

They genuinely care about the village, running regular coffee mornings to raise money for a variety of different charities and always happy to support any village events. Village news is always in the parish magazine, but as this only comes out once a month. Cakebreads is always hot off the press with any vital information which is put up in their window the next day.

In the summer there are benches and tables in the small courtyard outside the shop, but in the winter there is not enough room in the shop to provide catering on the same scale. Barbara has still managed to create a small table and three stools for any one, who on a wild winters day wants to rest a while from the storm.

Also this small oasis tucked away in the shop provides a service for any of the elderly villagers who may not be able to drive any more, but still want get out and have a chat and a light lunch while observing any folk coming in to the shop. They are also able to get any vital village news at the same time.

Barbara Cakebread presides over the shop with a cheery welcome for visitors and locals alike. In the summer the shop is buzzing, with pasties flying off the shelves to eat on the beach, doughnuts to enjoy on the quay, and all the other supplies needed for a Cornish holiday. One of our special treats on a summer morning is a Cakebreads breakfast outside on the patio.

Situated at the side of the shop it is the perfect spot to people watch while enjoying the best fried breakfast ever. It may not be as trendy as some places in Cornwall, but watching the world go by, getting the local gossip and planning the rest of the day takes some beating, trendy or not.

The coastal path runs up beside the community café, another perfect location to look out over the beach and watch harbour life. Keep going up the path, and it leads up and along to Vault beach, with the Dodman in the distance.

One spring morning we were lured up the path to Vault by the report of a whale stranded on the beach. I have to admit that I was dubious, but once we arrived and marched along the sand I could see it was indeed true, there it lay spread out across the beach at least thirty feet long. It was dead, a casualty of the sea, we wondered if it had died at sea or been washed up in the storms. Nobody knew what to do with it, it was far too big to get a line on and tow out to sea again, so there it stayed. There were various suggestions but in the end nature took over.

Gradually the great carcass began to disintegrate and was absorbed back into the sand. It had been a marvelous nature lesson for the local children, to actually see one of the great mammals of the sea so close was awe inspiring, yet sad but a natural introduction to the circle of life and death.

As we toiled up the steep path above the beach I remembered

another casualty of the sea which had a happier ending

. One sunny morning I took our dog Bengi down to the beach for a

quick run before going to work.

Bengi went running ahead as usual, to the edge of the water.

He suddenly stopped and came back to me.

I took a few steps and then I saw it, a seal just on the water's edge.

I approached slowly, usually, seals rush back into the water

immediately.

This one didn't move.

Keeping Bengi behind me, I crept closer, until I was right beside it, I

could see that it was only a young one, it lay on the wet sand,

helpless.

I could hear its rapid breathing. It made no attempt to move, but just

lay there obviously in great distress.

I was at a loss, what could I do?

Then something in the sea, caught my eye. I looked around and a

seal's head popped up just in front of me, and I could see brown eyes

staring at me.

Then it was gone. I debated what to do, this was before the days of mobile phones, and I had a class to teach that afternoon. Bengi was still apprehensive keeping a safe distance between him and the snuffling seal. I pondered, it was too big to get back into the sea. We walked further along the sand and then finally turned around. I was really hoping that the young seal had made it back into the water, but as we got near I could see that it was still there.

I glanced out to sea and there was the other one, even closer now, a much larger head watching me.

The penny suddenly dropped, it was the mother, who had headed her baby onto the beach and was watching to see what happened. Now you may call me a romantic fool but why was the young seal right at the beginning of the beach where it was sure to be found, and why would any other seal stay so close for so long?

It was clear to me that what I was experiencing was the power of maternal love.

I felt like shouting 'It's alright I will go and ring for help,' but instead Bengi and I hurried up the path and got onto the Seal Sanctuary down at Gweek.

I explained the situation, leaving out the watching mother seal bit of the story, I wanted to be taken seriously. They were busy they said, they were undertaking refurbishment, but they would send help. It would probably have to be taken up to West Hatch in Somerset.

'Can you meet us at the top?' they wanted to know.

I had to explain that I was in at college that afternoon and so could not be there, but I gave directions and put the phone down.

I had done my best.

  Later that afternoon when I got back from work I headed down the path to Vault beach. There was no sign of the seal so I asked a friend who lived in the old farm house at the top.

'Yes,' she said, a van had come with a stretcher the seal had been carried up the cliff, and it was going to West Hatch

I was impressed, the cliff path is steep and long and the young seal was quite hefty. I immediately rung West Hatch, and was told he was settling in well.

Apparently, he had picked up a virus, hence the runny nose and snuffles, he would be fine.

I went to bed that night happy, it was good to know that here in Cornwall we care for our wild life, help is there if needed.

  The seal sanctuary, was first started by a couple who lived beside the sea, and finding baby seals washed up by the violent storms began rescuing them, building a small pool , in their back garden. The idea finally grew into the major rescue center that it is today.

CHAPTER TWENTY

HIDDEN CORNWALL

Cornwall has something for ever one, from the sweeping beaches of the wild north coast to the more gentle, hidden coves of the south. With its rivers and moors and history of smugglers and miners, farmers and fishermen, it is also holds another attraction, it is a land of secrets.

I realized this some years ago, when we went to a New Year's party, and met a vibrant young man who had only recently moved down to the county. He began describing some lost gardens which he had found, and which were part of a big estate called Heligan.

His plan, he said, was to bring them back to life and he was passionate about how he wanted to achieve this goal. I listened with interest, I had heard my mother talk about Heligan estate, years ago, she had been great friends with the steward's daughter and had remembered stealing into the big house to gaze at the pictures on the walls and wonder what was under the huge dust sheets covering the furniture.

Also, we had another connection with Heligan. When the contents of the big house were sold at auction, we were about to get married, and it seemed a perfect chance to have a look around the old house and pick up a bargain. We had wandered around marveling at the size of the rooms and loving the panoramic views leading down the valley to Mevagissey and the sea. We finished up buying a large roll of pale pink carpet, which easily covered two rooms of our newly renovated old farm house, Church Park.

The young man we had met was called Tim Smitt, and later when talking about his enthusiastic plans Rob had casually said, 'we can go up and have a look at the gardens if you like.'
The opportunity presented itself a week later when we decided to take some friends with us to go and discover for ourselves these so called 'lost gardens.'

When we got there, we found that the way was barred   Although the house had been converted into flats, the gardens remained a complete wilderness, and as far as we could see there was no apparent way in, but we had not reckoned with Rob's local knowledge. He led us down a lane at the side of the gardens, and coming to a hedge on the way down proceeded to jump up, push down the wire fence, and invite us all to become trespassers. Eager to discover what Tim had become so excited about we all climbed over the hedge and found ourselves in what seemed to me to be a complete jungle.

The huge trees seemed to reach up to the sky and blocked out any light, great bushes

barred the way encased in weeds and brambles.

'Look up,' said Rob, and as I followed his gaze I found that I was looking at what seemed to me to be a gigantic fern which was reaching straight up to the sky, it was like nothing I had ever seen before. Just below it was an enormous plant like a gigantic rhubarb.

'Its a jungle,' I whispered.

I felt totally enclosed, as though the trees were gathering around us hemming us in, the bushes grabbing at our clothes as we tried to beat a way through.

The gardens were banning our way, not wanting to be disturbed from their hundred years sleep.

   The odour of damp earth and mildew hung on the air, I had the over whelming feeling that not only were we trespassing, but that we were encroaching on a lost moment in time which was not ours to disturb.

What we did not realize at the time was that we had stumbled upon the 'lost valley,' which would later be restored to its previous days of glory, and that the rest of the sleeping gardens would be woken to delight future generations.

The Lost Gardens were a revelation, but there was more to come.

 When our friend Mike Shepherd told us that his theatre company was going to perform down at the Minack, near Porthcurno, we didn't know what to expect.

I remember asking 'where is this Minack?'

   He proceeded to explain that Minack was an open air theatre perched on the side of a cliff, and had been the brain child of an eccentric woman called Rowena Cade. She had, had a vision, and with the help of her trusty gardener set about realizing her dream. She hauled rocks and mixed cement and created a unique venue similar to a Roman amphitheatre, and situated in a sublime setting, looking out to sea and across the bay towards Logan Rock.

Because Mike was an ardent cricketer, Rob was easily persuaded to pack us all into the car and experience some open air. Cornish culture. No Cornish expedition is 'proper job,' without a pasty and I set to with a will, to make four huge pasties. The kids were old enough now to appreciate a bit of culture, and so with a group of friends all in convoy, and all driving old family cars which were only used to doing local trips, we all set off.

When we pulled into the car park on the top of the cliff I realized that the setting was unique. I looked down over the seating area and out to an azure blue sea, with the sun low in the water and a fishing boat followed by a flock of hungry gulls, making its way back home. I knew without doubt that we were in for a memorable experience. Mike had filled me in with the amazing history of the theatre, the story of this lady Rowena Cade and her vision. When I actually saw the sheer scale and beauty of the place, I was amazed. How could one woman achieve so much, what an inspiration to sheer determination to follow your dreams.

Built of carved granite with the stage reaching out over the ocean and the sound of the waves breaking onto the rocks below, it was awe inspiring. The show couldn't have been more fitting, 'Long John Silver' and Kneehigh, young, talented and full of action made the most of the environment. We sat mesmerized, then to top it all, the Scillonian, returning from the Isles of Scilly, sailed gently past and we all craned our necks looking for the skull and cross bones flying behind her.

The interval was greeted with the sound of bottles being opened and pasties being unwrapped, people produced rugs to wrap around their legs and proceeded to settle down for the second half of the show. The actors began again, Long John Silver hobbled out onto the stage and there was a gasp from the audience. People began pointing out to sea.

'What on earth is it?' I asked.

Rob gazed out and pointed, and then I saw what everyone one was looking at. A pod of dolphins appeared in the sea below, one suddenly jumped out of the water in front of the stage. Then another jumped even higher, the audience were speechless, was it all part of the show, it seemed too good to be true, could it really be happening.

The actors gave up trying to compete and we all watched the second show 'the dance of the dolphins.' No one could believe what they were seeing, first the fishing boats in the setting sun, then the Scillonian making her way back from the islands, and now a pod of dolphins, out doing them all. It was an evening to remember for ever.

When we plodded up the winding paths to the car park we were over whelmed at what we had seen. Another secret of Cornwall revealed to those lucky enough to have been in the right place at the right time.

One of our favourite beaches is Great Perhaver, just a stone's throw by sea from Gorran Haven, but that short distance hides a variety of challenges.

The only access is by boat, and landing on the beach when the sea is calm can be perfect, trying to land when the wind is southerly can be more tricky. We have been caught out many times at Great

Perhaver, landing on a blissfully sunny morning spending the day swimming and building camp fires, only to be faced by a mischievous sea whipped up by the southerly wind behind our backs. The now daunting waves just waiting to swamp the boat as we attempt to load up all our beach gear and children, and head home to the safety of the Haven beach, a short row away.

In spite of this, the isolation and of the place still beckons. There are huge rocks to hide under and climb, and when the tide is out there is a great stretch of sand ideal for beach cricket. There are pools deep enough to catch small fish and shrimps, and crabs to be found under submerged rocks. The mussels which cling to the rocks are enormous, and the beach combing will always provide some unusual treasures to take home.

There is a special place where we all love to swim, a kind of pool which is enclosed by a pinnacle of rocks. Swimming one idyllic sunny morning I noticed a huge iron ring attached to the top of one of the rocks.

'What's this?' I yelled to Rob, who was still out in the boat messing around.

He completed his vital boat maintenance, i.e. stowing away the life jackets and dived over the side to join me.

'Oh, that's just to tie up the boats.'

'What boats?' I asked.

'The boats coming to the mine,' was the answer.

'If you look down you can see the remains of an old sheer wheel.' I gazed up at the iron ring and the jagged rocks, I had no idea what he was talking about

. When we got back onto the beach I delved further, Rob is one of the strong silent types, talking is not one of his strong points, he has to be cajoled into it.

Once he got going, the tale he had to tell was fascinating. The old rocks I had been swimming around had been the basis of a landing stage. There had been an old ochre mine in the field above us. The sailing ships had moored up alongside the iron and wood landing stage waiting to be loaded with the valuable yellow ochre which would then be transported to London.

Ochre, I discovered was the pigment used by artists to make yellow paint.

Later in the old photos of the village, I discovered a marvellous photo of an old sailing ship tied up alongside waiting to be loaded.

I wondered if any of the old masters had been painted with ochre

from the mine field above Great Perhaver, surely some had made its

way down to the Newlyn School of artists, had Stanhope Forbes

used our ochre .

How did they get on with the south winds and the sudden rollers

which appeared from no where. Did they get swamped like us, or

were they better sailors.?

I have to say I did not envy them, at least we had an engine.

They were relying only on their seamanship and their sails. It was

yet another example of hidden Cornwall.

CHAPTER TWENTY ONE

THE CALL OF CORNWALL

I have a friend called Dolores, we seem to have known each other

for ever. Our children went to the village playgroup together, then on to Gorran Primary school at the top of the hill opposite the cricket field, and finally on the school bus lumbering down the winding Cornish lanes to The Roseland School in the little village of Tregony.

The two families grew up together, sharing sunlit after school afternoons on the beach, to late evening barbecues on Hemmick. Dolores is a true local, born in Mevagissey she moved to Gorran Haven when she got married, (but her heart was always in Mevagissey) and is also a member of the same family clan as my mother, who emigrated to Plymouth, the Hunkins.. I say clan, because when I moved down to Cornwall and began to understand the intricacies of these huge Cornish families the sheer volume of each was breath taking.

Please note that I use the word emigrate purposely. Emigration has played such an important part in the history of Cornwall. I think of the miners who burrowed deep into the earth of west Cornwall seeking the valuable tin hidden below.

They also mined under the sea, where they could hear the sound of the rocks, on the ocean floor above them, being shifted by the gigantic waves just above their heads, as they dug and blasted for the precious tin

. Mined at great risk, to keep body and soul together and reap rich rewards for the prosperous mine owners.

Mining was a precarious business, life was cheap, and so many of those early miners decided to seek their fortune overseas. Thousands of Cornish miners left the land of their birth and took their first steps into the great unknown, they ended up all over the world.

There are Cornish pasties in Mexico, courtesy of those early miners who dug and sweated in holes in Australia, Canada, New Zealand to name just a few.

There is a saying, 'where there is a hole in the ground, you will find a Cornishman.'

Those early immigrants left their towns and villages to search for a better life for their families, many found it, some died, looking, but in all these countries there are strong Cornish connections.

So why use the word emigrate for the ones like my mother's family who only made it across the Tamar. How can it compare with those who travelled across the oceans of the world searching for a better life.?

I think that it does compare, in a way

. Fifty or five thousand miles, the effect to a degree, was the same. They had all left the tight knit communities that they had grown up in, and the county of their birth to forge a new life. The fascinating thing, is that so many, kept their links with home. Those Cornish towns and villages with their chapels and celebrations had gripped the hearts of those born to the sound of the sea and called them back often over the generations, to the land of their ancestors.

My mother's family had emigrated to Plymouth, and were lucky to be able to get back to Mevagissey and keep their links with the village alive.

I had been brought up with stories of 'Mevagissey Feast' and chapel teas and endless tales of many Hunkin relatives.

I already understood that the Hunkins had been very prolific and that I had second , third and fourth Hunkin cousins all over Mevagissey.

So when one morning I had a phone call from another Hunkin, my friend Dolores, saying

'How about coming into Mevagissey this afternoon, one of our distant cousins has produced the family tree, let's go and see it'.

I was hooked.

What I had not bargained for was the amazing story which we discovered that fateful afternoon. This was in the days when searching for long lost relatives was a relatively new past time and we had no idea about what to expect. When we got there, we discovered that the so called 'family tree' was more of a rampant forest taking up an entire wall, but fascinating.

'Look at this,' Dolores enthused, and we both peered at one particular group

. As I read the story of a long lost member of the Hunkin clan, a Matthew Hunkin, I could hardly believe my eyes. It was a perfect script for a film.

There was adversity, adventure and finally romance, plus a happy ending, what more could you want?

And the best bit, it was all true, fully documented.

Matthew Hunkin was born in 1815,and it seemed to me that it was possible that he had been one of the unfortunate Mevagissey fishermen who had been press ganged into joining the King's navy

I felt immediate sympathy with this long lost cousin. Knowing the winding streets and secret alleyways of Mevagissey I felt indignant on his behalf that he had not managed to evade the marauding soldiers, and had been spirited away from all that he knew to serve on a stinking, ship, risking life and limb when all he wanted was a normal life in his home village.

That could have been the end of the story, when in fact it turned out to be only the beginning

Matthew Hunkin was a true Cornishman, with a strong independent spirit. His ship sailed to South America and as it neared the island of Samoa he saw an opportunity to escape.

The ship anchored in the bay, and when he looked out at the golden beaches and waving palm trees he made a choice, and he chose Samoa.

One quiet night when the ships company were all asleep, he slipped out of his hammock, and stealthily made his way up onto the deck avoiding the man at arms

Grapping his chance, he slid noiselessly into the water and began his swim to freedom.

Records of the time prove that he was never caught, he settled on the island of Samoa where he married the chief's daughter,

Fatumalama, in1838 and raised a large family, never returning to Mevagissey. What a story, and there was more to come, once again Dolores made one of her amazing phone calls this time to say,

'Guess who I have got here all the way from Samoa?'

'No idea,' I said.

'It's Tui and Seme descendents of Matthew Hunkin, bring Michael, he'll love it.'

My son Michael loves history, especially Cornish history and he was as delighted as I was when we were ushered into Dolores sitting room to be introduced to Tui and Seme Hunkin all the way from Hawaii.

Beautiful people, they had wanted to come down to Cornwall and see for themselves the tiny fishing village which their ancestor had left behind back in1830. Had he been one of the fishermen running for his life through the winding alleys and streets of Mevagissey, I like to think so.

How strange that so many years later his story had been handed down, and his descendants were now back in the county of his birth.

Later when looking at records from the London Missionary Society I discovered that Matthew had been paid twenty pounds a year where he was described as a 'reformed or runaway sailor' who would preach the gospel on the behalf of the Society.

This all led to confirm my suspicion that the term 'reformed or runaway sailor' referred to him 'jumping ship.'

Records from the society also describe how in1840 Matthew Hunkin was able to arouse the people of Manua and a church was formed there.

So, our runaway sailor who jumped ship became an inspiring preacher who founded his own church.

Tui and Seme loved Mevagissey and before they left, they went to the end of Mevagissey quay and kissed the ground taking home with them a piece of the cliff to put on Matthew's grave which lies on a headland, on the island which gave him sanctuary Samoa.

After that first visit from Samoa other members of the family came back, we found out what a large extended Hunkin clan there was in both Samoa and Hawaii,

One of the clan is a member of the House of Representatives for Hawaii and is in contact with his Cornish side of the family having been given one of the black and gold Cornish rugby shirts which hangs proudly in his office in Washington.

Some years ago a fishing boat, sailed quietly out of Mevagissey harbour it was carrying the ashes of another Hunkin from across the water, an uncle of mine who I had heard of but never met. We shared the same grandfather so it was appropriate that the ashes were carried on a fishing boat.

Geoff's father Gilbert had emigrated to London, so Geoff's visits to Mevagissey would have been brief.

Geoff joined the Air Force as a pilot in World War Two, and after the war,qualified as a mining engineer. He travelled all over the world and only visited Mevagissey a few times,

The interesting thing is that when he died he wanted his ashes to be scattered in the waters of Mevagissey bay, where his grandfather had fished so many years before. How appropriate then that his last journey was in a fishing boat.

Cornwall it seems, never really lets go of her own, they all come back some sooner than later

My own twins once they were adults, both longed to get back to the county of their birth, as do so many others of all generations.

There are Cornish associations all over the world all remembering their Cornish roots, all making pasties all flying the Cornish flag. It seems that Cornwall will always call to its own down the years, not only to those lucky enough to have been born here, but also to those who have loved the county, and made it their own.

This little end of Britain, almost surrounded by water, with its rugged coast and wind swept moors, its winding rivers and hidden creeks, possesses a magic which will never fade. This Cornwall.

Printed in Great Britain
by Amazon

41850036R00102